NORTH ISLAND
weekend tramps

NORTH ISLAND
weekend tramps

SHAUN BARNETT

craig potton publishing

For Tom, Lee and Lexi and the tramps we'll do together

First published in 2002 by
Craig Potton Publishing
98 Vickerman Street, PO Box 555, Nelson, New Zealand
www.craigpotton.co.nz

This revised edition first published in 2008

© Text and photographs: Shaun Barnett/Black Robin Photography
© Maps: Geographx

ISBN 978 1 877333 95 8

Printed by Tien Wah Press, Singapore

ACKNOWLEDGEMENTS

The idea for this book originated with Rob Brown, my co-author on *Classic Tramping in New Zealand*. Rob suggested there was a need for guidebooks on weekend length tramps, and Craig Potton Publishing approached me with the idea of writing one for the North Island. Another friend, Nick Groves, has written a companion volume for the South Island.

I'd like to thank a number of people who were great companions in the hills while I researched this book, namely Daryl Ball, Angela Barnett, Grant Barnett, Rob Brown, Andy Dennis, Margot Ferrier, John Fitzgerald, Tony Gates, David Hall, Dave Hansford, Marieke Hilhorst, Debbie Hoare, Stephen Hormann, Andrew Lynch, Chris Maclean, Sarah-Jane Mariott, Geoff Norman, John Ombler, Darryn Pegram, Jock Phillips, Bruce Postill, Jane Reeves, John Rhodes, Jim Ribiero, Jason Roxburgh, Roger Smith, Mark Stanton, Tania Stanton, Tom Stanton-Barnett, Louise Thornley and Hayden Titchener.

Thank you to the following Department of Conservation staff who advised me on specific chapters: Wayne Boness, Stephen Hormann, Bruce Postill, Jason Roxburgh and George Taylor. Other people who generously shared their local knowledge were Liz and Mike Sampson (Auckland), and Peter McKellar (Rotorua). I am also grateful to Paora Brooking, from Ngati Porou, for permission to reproduce a picture of their whakairo on Mt Hikurangi.

Lastly, heartfelt thanks to Roger Smith of Geographx (www.geographx.co.nz) for his wonderful maps, and the team at Craig Potton Publishing – particularly Robbie Burton, Tina Delceg and Arnott Potter – for many years of support, encouragement and hard work behind the scenes.

CONTENTS

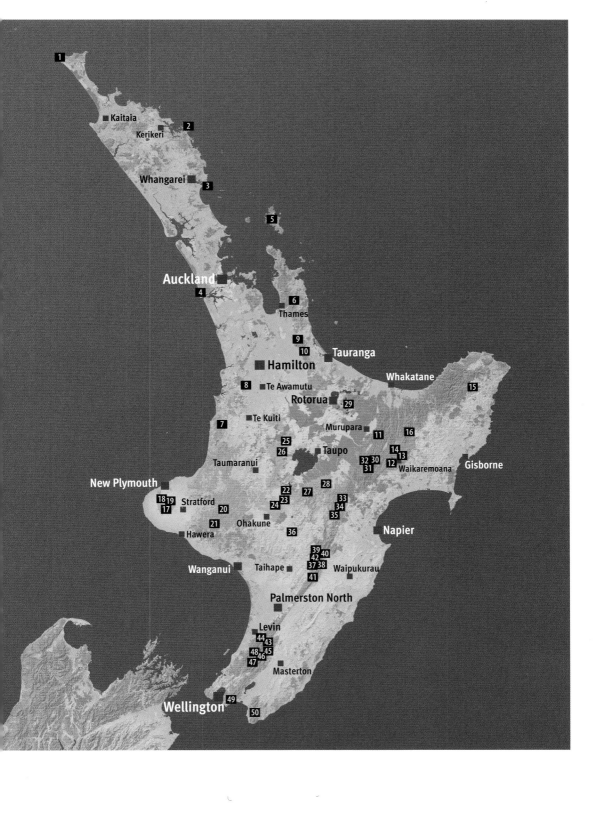

Kaitaia

Kerikeri

Whangarei

Auckland

Thames

Hamilton

Te Awamutu

Rotorua

Whakatane

Te Kuiti

Murupara

Taumaranui

Taupo

Waikaremoana

Gisborne

New Plymouth

Stratford

Ohakune

Hawera

Napier

Wanganui

Taihape

Waipukurau

Palmerston North

Levin

Masterton

Wellington

INTRODUCTION

While many people look to the South Island for tramping trips, in a number of ways the North Island offers a greater range of experiences for trampers. Certainly the diversity of forests and the presence of active volcanic landscapes distinguish North Island tramps from those on the 'mainland'. Another advantage of North Island tramps is the generally low numbers of sandflies – something that certainly cannot be said of the South Island! Furthermore, the majority of New Zealanders do indeed live in the North Island, and aside from their annual leave are left with only weekends in which to head for the hills.

This guidebook is intended for trampers who are looking for ideas and information on a range of weekend-length tramps in the North Island. I've taken the liberty of including two longer tramps, primarily because of their popularity as 'long weekend' trips, especially at Easter. Aside from these (the Matemateaonga Walkway in Whanganui National Park and the Lake Waikaremoana Great Walk in Te Urewera National Park), most of the remaining tramps described can be accomplished by moderately fit trampers over the course of a normal weekend. A few of the harder trips do require a very good level of fitness if they are to be completed in two days, although they can more easily be tackled over three.

Tramps in this book have been chosen from the length and breadth of the North Island, reflecting a range of terrain, natural history and level of difficulty. Included are tramps in the kauri forests of the Coromandel, Great Barrier Island and the Kaimai Range; and coastal walks at Auckland's Waitakere Ranges and Cape Brett, Cape Reinga and Peach Cove in Northland. The majestic podocarp forests of Whirinaki and Pureora are unique to the North Island, while volcanic landscapes also provide distinctly North Island tramping experiences – this book includes tramps at Mt Taranaki and Tongariro National Park.

Several of the tramps include a chance to climb the highest peak in an area: Kaweka J in Kaweka Forest Park, Mangaweka in Ruahine Forest Park, Mt Manuoha in Te Urewera National Park, Mt Hikurangi in Raukumara Forest Park, Mt Matthews in Rimutaka Forest Park, Mitre in Tararua Forest Park and Mt Taranaki in Egmont National Park. Yet others follow historic routes, including the Waitawheta Valley and Pinnacles Hut tramps, as well as the Matemateaonga Track. On all of the tramps you'll encounter a range of native animals and birds.

A high proportion of the tramps cross a mixture of terrain, passing through bush, crossing rivers and ascending tops. Some of the walks are very well known, including the Tongariro Crossing, Southern Crossing and Lake Waikaremoana Great Walk. Others are less well known, notably Leitchs Clearing, Waihaha Hut and Waioeka Forest.

The first two editions (2002 and 2004) included 43 tramps. In this expanded edition, three of the shorter tramps (Kapiti Island, Cape Kidnappers and Arahaki Lagoon) have been removed – and are now covered in *Day Walks in New Zealand* (2007). These have been replaced by 10 new weekend tramps, bringing the total up to 50. More tramps in the upper half of the North Island have been introduced to partially redress the imbalance of previous editions, which were more heavily weighted towards the lower North Island.

LENGTH AND DIFFICULTY

Each tramp is classified according to difficulty, which readers should note depends very much on conditions. Wet weather could very well turn a medium river trip into a hard one, while winter snow may transform a medium or hard tops trip into one that requires mountaineering skills. When selecting a tramp it is also important to take the abilities of all party members into consideration.

Each walk is classified into 'easy', 'medium', 'hard' or 'mountaineering' grades. On an 'easy' walk you can expect gentle terrain, well-marked tracks, few if any river crossings, and walking times of less than three to four hours per day. On a 'medium' trip you may have river crossings, and there could be steep sections of track or some travel on unmarked, open tops. Travel times could be five to six hours per day. A 'hard' tramp will involve longer days, possibly eight hours or more, and is likely to feature some unmarked travel and considerable river crossing.

Only one 'mountaineering' trip is included in this book: the ascent of Taranaki. While in summer this can be a simple scree climb, in most other seasons tackling Taranaki will require some mountaineering knowledge, as well as the use of an ice axe and crampons. However, by far the majority of the tramps fall into the easy and medium categories, with just a few in the hard category.

Where appropriate, options for either shortening or lengthening tramps have been suggested, allowing for changes in weather and varying levels of fitness. For example, the Sunrise Hut tramp can be spread over two longer days when a traverse of Te Atuaopara-para to Waipawa Forks Hut is undertaken, or simply accomplished as a day trip just to the hut itself.

KEEPING INFORMATION UP TO DATE

Although every effort has been made to ensure that information in this guide is both correct and up to date, please remember that wild places change constantly. Floods alter rivers, volcanoes erupt from time to time and storms can devastate forests and tracks. Furthermore, the condition of tracks and huts varies according to how recently they have been maintained. For these reasons, it is advisable for trampers to check with local Department of Conservation (DOC) offices for updates. The relevant DOC telephone number has been given for each tramp, and the DOC website (www.doc.govt.nz) is also an excellent source of information.

MAPS

Each tramp in this book is accompanied by a 'bird's eye' map, which gives readers a superb three-dimensional view of the terrain. The maps indicate tracks, huts, bridges and major topographical features, but are not intended to be used for navigation – for this you should purchase a NZMS 260 series 1:50,000 topographical map. Details of the correct map(s) for the tramps are included in the 'fact file' at the beginning of each chapter.

Land Information New Zealand (LINZ) is completing a new range of maps – the Topo50 Map Series – which will cover the entire country using the New Zealand Geodetic

Datum (NZGD2000). These will replace the 260 series (which used NZGD49) in September 2009 (see www.linz.govt.nz). The website has an online facility to convert an old grid reference to one under the new projection.

Note that true left refers to the left bank of a river when facing downstream, and true right to the right bank.

HUTS AND HUT FEES

New Zealand's hut network – which includes over 950 back-country huts – is unique in the world, but requires your support if it is to be maintained. DOC charges modest fees for most huts, except for Basic huts and bivs which are free. Other hut categories include Serviced huts ($15 per night) and Standard huts ($5 per night). Charges vary for Great Walk huts. Youths aged 11–17 are half price, and children 10 and under are free.

Great Walk huts have heating and gas cooking facilities. Serviced Huts have heating facilities, an indoor sink and running water. Standard Huts usually just have mattresses and perhaps a woodstove or open fire. Basic huts or bivs may be just a simple shell, without even mattresses. Hut tickets can be purchased from most DOC offices and some information centres and retailers. Check out www.doc.govt.nz for further information.

For those doing a lot of tramping (say, spending more than 10–15 nights in a back-country hut per year), a good-value option is to purchase a Back-country Hut Pass. These cost $90 for adults and $45 for youths and allow the use of all Basic, Serviced and Standard huts. A 30 per cent discount on the Back-country Hut Pass is available to FMC-affiliated club members (see: www.fmc.org.nz).

HUT ETIQUETTE

At night or during bad weather, the hut forms the focus of the tramping experience and is part of the tradition of the New Zealand back country. A few simple courtesies make the experience an enjoyable one for all, even in a crowded hut.

Always make room for newcomers, even if the hut is nearing capacity. When the hut is full, consider using a tent if you have one. Inside, keep your gear tidy and contained, and try not to spread out too much. Remove wet boots before entering the hut to keep the floor clean and dry. Cook with ventilation. When leaving, make sure all benches and tables are clean, sweep the floor, close all windows and doors, and ensure you've replaced any firewood used. You won't go far wrong if you follow the rule, 'Leave the hut as you'd hope to find it'.

WATER AND CONSERVATION

Giardia is present in many back-country waterways, but there are still significant areas where you can safely drink straight from the stream. If in doubt, carry water treatments, boil the water for five minutes or use a water filter. Do not use soap or detergent in lakes or streams, and where possible use toilets. If there is no longdrop, go to the toilet at least 100 metres from water sources and bury your waste in a shallow 'cat scrape'. When camping take care not to pitch your tent in a fragile area, and refrain from hacking poles out of saplings. Have consideration for the environment: don't take away anything natural and don't leave anything unnatural. Carry out all your rubbish and any you find. Avoid lighting fires when they are unnecessary (in summer) or during a fire ban. In some areas (such as the bushline) dead firewood is in very short supply and should be burned only when absolutely necessary. Dismantle outdoor fireplaces after use.

EQUIPMENT, SAFETY AND FURTHER INFORMATION

There is not the scope in this book to give a detailed description of equipment and safety, but a brief list of what should be carried for a typical weekend tramp is as follows: sleeping bag, billy, burner, fuel, warm woolly hat, sunhat, gloves, raincoat, warm jersey or fleece, two pairs of polypropylene or woollen long-johns, two wool or polypropylene tops, a pair of shorts, first-aid kit, mug, plate, utensils, two pairs of warm socks, map, compass, torch, sunscreen, candles, matches and enough food for the duration of the trip plus a few extra snacks and one extra meal. For some trips you might like to take a tent, or at least a flysheet and sleeping mat. In winter, you may need to add ice axe, crampons, sunglasses, more warm gear, extra fuel and food. You should leave your intentions, including possible bad-weather alternatives, with a trusted friend who can, in the event of your party becoming overdue, be relied upon to contact the Police Search and Rescue (phone 111 and ask for Search and Rescue). Remember that rivers are the biggest hazard in the back country and cause the most deaths. You should therefore be well versed in the current Mountain Safety Council river-crossing techniques and have practised these before you need to use them in a real situation. Many tramping clubs offer introductory courses to river crossing, bushcraft and navigation. If you would like to join a tramping club, check out the Federated Mountain Club website (www.fmc.org.nz).

Beginners who would like more information about the 'how' of tramping should consult Sarah Bennett and Lee Slater's excellent book *Don't Forget Your Scroggin* (2007) and the *Bushcraft Manual* published by the Mountain Safety Council (www.mountainsafety. org.nz).

Those who would like to know more about the history of tramping and the outdoors in New Zealand can find information in *Te Ara*, the online encyclopaedia of New Zealand (www. teara.govt.nz). Click on the section called 'The Bush' which includes excellent stories and pictures about tramping, mountaineering, tracks, outdoor people and natural history.

Finally – happy tramping!

REFERENCES AND FURTHER READING

Allen, S. *Bushcraft Manual, Outdoor Skills for the NZ Bush*, 4th edition (Wellington: Mountain Safety Council, 2006)

Armitage, D. (ed.) *Great Barrier Island* (Christchurch: Canterbury University Press, 2001)

Barnett, S. & Brown, R. *Classic Tramping in New Zealand* (Nelson: Craig Potton Publishing, 1999)

Barnett, S. *Tramping in New Zealand* (Nelson: Craig Potton Publishing, 2006)

Barnett, S. *Day Walks in New Zealand* (Nelson: Craig Potton Publishing, 2007)

Bates, Arthur P. 'The Waitotara Valley, a few background notes' from *The Wanganui Tramper*, Oct–Dec 1989

Bennett, S. & Slater, L. *Don't Forget Your Scroggin, A How-to Handbook for New Zealand Tramping* (Nelson: Craig Potton Publishing, 2007)

Dawson, J. & Lucas, R. *Nature Guide to the New Zealand Forest* (Auckland: Godwit, 2000)

Diamond, J & Hayward, B. *Waitakere Kauri, A Pictorial History of the Kauri Timber Industry in the Waitakere Ranges* (Auckland: Lodestar Press, 1980)

Department of Conservation *Guide to the Waitawheta Valley, Kaimai-Mamaku Forest Park* (Rotorua: DOC Bay of Plenty Conservancy, 1993)

Department of Conservation *Tracks Through Time, Moments In History of the Kaimai-Mamaku Forest Park* (Rotorua: DOC Bay of Plenty Conservancy, 1997)

Dreaver, A. *An Eye for Country – the Life and Work of Leslie Adkin* (Wellington: Victoria University Press, 1997)

Gibbons, A. & Sheehan, G. *Leading Lights, Lighthouses of New Zealand* (Christchurch: Hazard Press, 1991)

Greenaway, R. *The Restless Land – Stories of Tongariro National Park* (Turangi: DOC/Tongariro Natural History Society, 1998)

Harvey, B. *Rolling Thunder, The Spirit of Karekare* (Auckland: Exisle Publishing, 2001)

Maclean, C. *Tararua – The Story of a Mountain Range* (Wellington: Whitcombe Press, 1994)

Molloy, L. & Potton, C. *New Zealand's Wilderness Heritage* (Nelson: Craig Potton Publishing, 2007)

Ombler, K. *National Parks and Other Wild Places of New Zealand* (Cape Town: Struik New Holland Publishers, 2001)

Pickering, M. *A Tramper's Journey* (Nelson: Craig Potton Publishing, 2004)

Potton, C. *Classic Walks of New Zealand* (Nelson: Craig Potton Publishing, 2004)

Spearpoint, G. *Waking to the Hills* (Auckland: Reed-Methuen, 1985)

NZ Wilderness is a monthly magazine that regularly features weekend tramps, as well as stories on conservation, exploration, mountain biking, sea kayaking, climbing and natural history (www.wildernessmag.co.nz).

Useful websites:

www.doc.govt.nz   www.mountainsafety.org.nz
www.fmc.org.nz   www.tramper.co.nz
www.teara.govt.nz   www.geographx.co.nz

Trampers on the Whanahuia Range, Ruahine Forest Park

Cape Reinga Coastal Walkway

Duration 2 days

Grade Easy

Times Tapotupotu Bay camping area to Cape Reinga: 2–2.5 hours. Cape Reinga to Herangi Hill: 2 hours. Side trip to Cape Maria van Diemen: 90 minutes return. Herangi Hill to Twilight Beach: 1.5 hours. Twilight Beach to Te Paki Stream roadend: 4–5 hours.

Map M02 North Cape

Access From Kaitaia take SH 1 almost as far north as far as it goes. About 3 km shy of Cape Reinga turn off the sealed road and follow the gravel Tapotupotu Road for 2.5 km to its end at a camping area. Allow 90 minutes to drive the 112 km from Kaitaia. As the tramp ends at Te Paki Stream Road a car juggle is required; for a fee local operators can arrange this for you.

Alternative Route Those wanting a longer trip can begin from Kapowairua at Spirits Bay, which would add another 8 hours to the trip.

Information DOC Kaitaia Area Office, Ph 09 408 6014

The Cape Reinga Coastal Walkway is one of the longest walkways in the country, and also forms the starting point for Te Araroa – the New Zealand trail – which spans the entire length of the country to Bluff. This weekend tramp explores the most scenic portion of the walkway, beginning at Tapotupotu Bay, and ending at the magnificent Te Paki sand dunes. It's arguably the most spectacular coastal tramp in the North Island.

As there are no huts, trampers will need to carry a tent, and during summer should take plenty of water, as some of the streams can become unreliable. A filter could be handy, or plenty of burner fuel for boiling questionable water.

The tramp begins at Tapotupotu Bay, a delightful sandy beach fringed by pohutukawa, where there is a basic DOC campsite ($7.50/night, toilets, showers and water). At the western end of the beach, the track begins a climb onto a ridge above coastal cliffs, passing an old pa site en route. There are good views as far as Spirits Bay and the Surville Cliffs beyond.

After reaching the ridge crest (bear right at an unsignposted junction) the track descends steeply to Sandy Bay, which makes a pleasant place for a break. From Sandy Bay the track climbs solidly for 160 metres up a spur directly to Cape Reinga. Here you intercept the sealed path which leads to the lighthouse. No doubt you'll also encounter some of the 200,000 people who visit the cape each year, most of whom – happily for trampers – never venture off the path. Interpretation panels explain the significance of the cape.

Cape Reinga is of immense importance to Maori, who know it as Te Rerenga Wairua. Here, according to legend, the spirits of the deceased at last depart Aotearoa to begin the long journey back to the ancestral homeland of Hawaiki-A-Nui.

The lighthouse at the cape also forms one of New Zealand's most recognisable landmarks, and most New Zealanders harbour ambitions to visit it at some point in their lives. Contrary to popular opinion, the cape is not the northernmost tip of mainland New Zealand; the Surville Cliffs claim that record. Regardless, the cape can be a place of some beauty. Here the Tasman Sea and Pacific Ocean merge, and the sea often displays cross-currents and turbulence as it breaches the offshore reefs known as the Columbia Banks. Northward lie the Three Kings Islands, sometimes just dark spots beyond a sunlit sea; at other times rendered invisible by haze. The route towards Cape Maria van Diemen lies to the west.

Branching off the path to the lighthouse, the well-benched walkway begins a descent for 30 minutes beside coastal cliffs, down to the long sweep of Te Werahi Beach. At high tide, you may have to scramble around some rock platforms to stay out of the sea's reach. After following the coast southwards along the beach for an hour or so, the track crosses Te Werahi Stream (sometimes impassable after mid-tide) before heading inland up grassy slopes to colourful dunes beyond, dominated by the native sand plants pingao

Tramper on the track to Te Werahi Beach, Cape Reinga

and spinifex. A gentle climb on a poled route leads over the flanks of Herangi Hill (159 m) to a signposted track junction which offers fine views of Cape Maria van Diemen and Motuopao Island.

Between 5 and 2 million years ago, the whole area consisted of a small archipelago with volcanic origins, but in the last million years huge quantities of sand, deposited by oceanic currents, have created a connection with the mainland called a tombolo. Now, only the islands adjacent to Cape Maria van Diemen remain separated.

Sand patterns, Te Paki Recreation Reserve

Dutch explorer Abel Janszoon Tasman named Cape Maria van Diemen after the wife of the Governor of Batavia (a former province of Holland). He also christened the Three Kings Islands – a reference to the Bible's trio of wise men. On a good day the side track (90 minutes return) out to the cape proves rewarding. Poles lead down an extensive sand slope to the cape, through some rippled dunes where pingao and spinifex grow. From near the coast, a rough track climbs up through grass and flax to the lighthouse, which although a stubby cylinder with none of the charm of the lighthouse at Cape Reinga, does have excellent views.

Back at the track junction, the main walkway enters coastal shrublands, dominated by prostrate manuka and coastal flax, and traverses a broad ledge above the cliffs of Maungatiketike and Pitokuku points before descending towards Twilight Beach. From a signposted track junction, take the 5-minute walk to Twilight Beach. There's limited camping nearby, but no water.

From the junction it's possible to exit to Te Werahi Gate on State Highway 1 on a side track (allow 2–3 hours). But by far the most scenic option is to continue south from Twilight Beach to Te Paki.

The track follows Twilight Beach on firm sand for about 45 minutes. At the southern end of the beach, past a large orange marker, the track begins to climb towards Tehepouto Point. There's a small stream here (probably unreliable in summer) though the water quality possibly demands treatment or boiling. After about 10 minutes climbing, the track levels out and there are some good grassy sites for camping. Beyond, the track – which is a former farm road – traverses a flat-tish plateau flanked by the coastal cliffs of Tiriparepa (Scott) Point. Stubby, orange-capped marker posts indicate the route at a few junctions. Up until the 1960s much of North Cape, including Te Paki, was farmed, but now only about 2900 hectares remain in grass – some of which is visible inland. Now, regenerating coastal vegetation dominated by stunted manuka clings to the landscape, defiant against both the wind and salt-laden air.

At a final rise you gain a first view of Ninety Mile Beach, another famous Northland landmark, arcing southwards into the sea haze. The track descends steeply down a rutted section until reaching a boardwalk over a wetland, and then continues over a set of stairs for the final descent to Kahokawa Beach. This is actually the northernmost extent of Ninety Mile Beach. Large waves roll onto the sandy beach from the Tasman Sea, and the great curve of the beach provides a sense of expansiveness (although it's more like 90 kilometres, not miles). Good firm walking on the sand makes for fast progress down to Te Paki Stream. By now, 4WD vehicles, which can access the beach down Te Paki Stream, have probably interrupted your quiet walk.

It's only an hour's stroll upstream to the Te Paki roadend, but no sane tramper should miss the opportunity to explore the magnificent surrounding dunes. Te Paki is perhaps the most exquisite and extensive area of dunes in New Zealand; although parts of Stewart Island could lay claim to that boast too. Covering some 2000 hectares, and rolling inland for up to 4 kilometres, the dunes here are immense and one could almost get lost in them.

In places the sand ripples like archetypal desert terrain; in others rock outcrops or patches of pingao disrupt the sand-scape. Some of the dunes reach heights of 150 metres or so, and resemble small mountains. Great fun can be had running down them; but take care not to trample native vegetation.

The tramp concludes at a carpark adjacent to a grassy area with toilets.

Sunset at Cape Maria van Diemen, Northland

Cape Brett Scenic Reserve

Duration 2 days

Grade Medium–Hard

Times Rawhiti to Deep Water Cove Track junction: 4–6 hours. Junction to Cape Brett Hut (23 bunks, gas cookers, $12/night): 2–3 hours.

Map Q05 Bay of Islands

Access From Russell drive for 27 km on Russell, Kempthorne and Manawaora roads before turning left onto Rawhiti Road. Follow this for 7 km to Oke Bay, where the track is signposted on the right. Secure parking is available at 253 Rawhiti Road for $5. Cape Brett Hut is locked with a combination keypad, and you must pre-book the hut with DOC. In addition, the first part of the walk crosses private land administered by Cape Brett Walkways Ltd, and there is a track maintenance fee of $30 per person, also payable to DOC.

Alternative Routes Commercial operators based in Paihia run boat trips out to Cape Brett, and can arrange to drop you at a landing near the hut. It's also possible to be dropped off or picked up at Deep Water Cove.

Information DOC Bay of Islands/Pewhairangi Regional Visitor Centre, Ph 09 403 9005; Cape Brett Walkways Ltd, Ph 09 403 8823 (www. capebrettwalks.co.nz)

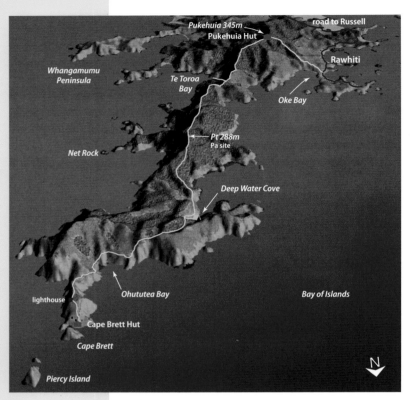

The impressive headland of Cape Brett, at the eastern boundary of the Bay of Islands, probes into the Pacific Ocean like an accusing finger. Seven small peaks form the spine of the peninsula, said by Maori to represent the seven waka in which the first Polynesians migrated to New Zealand.

Cape Brett is famed for the 'Hole in the Rock', a large natural archway in Piercy Island at the tip of the peninsula, through which boats take tourists. The cape also features a prominent lighthouse, and DOC has turned one of the former keepers' cottages into a very attractive hut. Trampers can reach this hut via the Cape Brett Walkway, which traverses the peninsula from the small coastal community of Rawhiti.

One might be fooled into thinking this is an easy coastal walk, but the rugged topography of the peninsula dictates otherwise, and reaching the hut requires a full day's walk on the sometimes testing 20-kilometre track. Note that there's very little water en route.

From Oke Bay the track leads up a series of stairs to where you get your first glimpse of the peninsula stretching away to the northeast. The track continues to climb steadily through regenerating forest typical of coastal Northland, including manuka, taraire, mahoe, silver fern, nikau palms and the occasional puriri. After crossing one small stream you reach the ridge crest at Pukehuia (345 m) where there is a shelter and water tank. These were installed for 'Project Crimson' workers undertaking possum control in an effort to protect the stands of coastal pohutukawa at threat from browsing. Travel is generally straightforward, and the track has recently been upgraded.

From Pukehuia, the track drops to a saddle where a side track branches off towards Te Toroa Bay. Further along there are occasional viewpoints overlooking the island-studded waters of the Bay of Islands. Near the narrowest point of the peninsula you reach an electrified possum-proof fence (installed in 1995), crossing from coast to coast. Eventually, hunters aim to eradicate possums from the peninsula tip, and this fence will ensure they don't reinvade. A gate through the fence gives access to the track beyond.

Further on, a convenient place for a break is found at a grassy knoll (288 m), an old pa site that overlooks Net Rock to the east. From the knoll, the track ambles down to a prominent junction. The left-hand branch leads to Deep Water Cove – a 30-minute side trip to a very pleasant and sheltered bay with idyllic turquoise waters.

Old lighthouse, Cape Brett, pictured before its recent restoration

Back at the track junction, continue straight on to pass into the Manawahuna/Cape Brett Scenic Reserve. After crossing a stream, the track ascends to a commanding lookout where the cape comes into dramatic profile. Some impressive cliffs fall into the sea here, and it's rather daunting to see how far there is yet to go. Sadly, much of the extensive stands of pohutukawa that once grew here are now dead, having been decimated in the days before possum control.

Cape Brett Hut, (restored lighthouse keeper's house), Cape Brett

After sidling through forest, the track crosses quite close to Ohututea Bay before beginning a steady haul up to a grassy saddle flanked by cliffs on both sides of the peninsula. From here the last kilometre or so traverses a razorback ridge, up to a knoll, from where there are astounding views of the lighthouse, the cape and Piercy Island beyond. The final stretch down to the hut has recently been restored by DOC and the Kerikeri Conservation Corp, who have removed much of the manuka and kikuyu grass that had grown over the historic track. Perched on a prominent flat, the hut overlooks the ocean.

Cape Brett Hut was beautifully restored in 1996 and has polished floorboards, gas cookers and 23 bunks. It's the only surviving cottage of three that once stood here to house the families of the lighthouse keepers. The old lighthouse itself was originally built in 1909 and became operational in 1910. When electrification came in the 1950s, the number of keepers was reduced to two, and then in 1978 the construction of a new automated light negated the need for any keepers at all. In 2008 DOC repainted the historic lighthouse, and replaced the heavy old wooden doors that were rotting.

Even with three families at the cape, it could be a lonely existence for both keepers and kin. The wife of one assistant keeper died in 1918, and he became so lonely that he sought a transfer from the Lighthouse Service. Then, during the 1930s, tension between families mounted to the extent that one keeper's wife suffered a breakdown.

Despite the hardships there must have been times when the keepers thanked their lucky stars for the lifestyle – perhaps during an exhilarating storm, or on a calm evening when they fished from the nearby shore. Even a brief stay in the hut gives some sense of what it must have been like to live here. On the cape's rare calm days it's possible to snorkel, and some trampers have even swum with dolphins.

For those not catching a boat back to Paihia, there is some comfort in knowing that the return plod along the walkway to Oke Bay is usually accomplished in less time as you will now be more familiar with the track.

Peach Cove & Te Whara Track

Duration 1–2 days

Grade Medium

Times Ocean Beach to Bream Head and Peach Cove Track junction: 2.5–3 hours. Side track to Peach Cove Hut (8 bunks, $10/night, locked): 20–30 minutes each way. Peach Cove Track junction to Urquharts Bay: 2.5–3 hours. Peach Cove Hut must be booked through DOC, who will supply a code for the keypad on the locked door.

Map R07 Whangarei

Access From Whangarei take Riverside Drive, Whangarei Heads Road and Ocean Beach Road to reach a DOC carpark at Ocean Beach, which has toilets and an information panel. Allow about 40 minutes to drive the 30 km from Whangarei. The Te Whara Track ends at Urquharts Bay, 5 km away from Ocean Beach by road.

Alternative Routes Trampers can approach Peach Cove Hut directly from Ocean Road (1 hour). Trampers can also extend their walk at the Urquharts Bay end by completing a loop track around Busby Head and the Smugglers Bay Track (add an extra 1–1.5 hours).

Information DOC Whangarei, Ph 09 470 3340; Bream Head Conservation Trust, www.breamheadtrust.org.nz

At the head of Whangarei Harbour several peaks rise monolithically, their sheerness and close proximity to the sea lending them a stature that belies their modest heights. At 475 metres, Bream Head/Te Whara is the highest of these, the eroded stump of a volcano that formed 20 million years ago; Manaia and Mt Lion are the other two prominent peaks.

Botanically, Bream Head is of national importance, containing Northland's largest remaining broadleaf–pohutukawa forest and some locally endemic species. Peach Cove lies on the seaward side of Bream Head, an idyllic sandy cove overhung by gnarled pohutukawa. A hut lies just back from the beach, set in a subtropical grove of trees. Due to its accessibility by boat, Peach Cove Hut is kept locked, but can be booked by trampers for overnight stays.

Overlooking Ocean Beach, Whangarei

As one of just seven back-country huts in Northland, it offers one of the few overnight tramping opportunities in the region.

While the quickest route to the hut on the Peach Cove Track takes little more than an hour, a more challenging and interesting tramp can be completed using the Te Whara Track. This follows the route of an historic Ngatiwai trail, linking Ocean Beach with Urquharts Bay, and traversing the summits of Bream Head and Lion Rock en route. Peach Cove is reached on a short side track off the main Te Whara Track.

Trampers must expect some steep and slippery terrain, on a well-marked but not formed tramping track. However, the rewards are outstanding views and superb sandy beaches, with much of historic interest too. As there is very little water en route, carry plenty with you, especially during summer.

From the carpark at Ocean Beach, head eastwards over the white sands for five minutes before picking up a track that climbs up grassy slopes. Views of the Bream Islands and the more distant Poor Knights Islands soon unfold. After about 40 minutes climbing, past a small lighthouse, the track reaches an old World War II naval radar station base built in 1942. This was one of several built around Northland and the Hauraki Gulf in anticipation of an attack by Japanese forces which never occurred. Once there was a bunkhouse with accommodation for up to 25 people. Although little remains of the station buildings now, the rusting radar is visible, tucked into the nearby bush with the dramatic rock spire known as the Old Woman beyond.

Beyond the historic station, the track enters forest and continues to climb until reaching the ridge crest near Bream Head. While well marked with orange triangles, this part of the track is steep, narrow and slippery in places. On the ridge crest, a side track leads

Peach Cove, Bream Head Scenic Reserve

up to a viewpoint on the head (475 m), but it will tempt only more agile trampers who have a good head for heights. On a good day you can see as far south as Cape Rodney, as far north as Cape Brett and across to the Coromandel Peninsula.

Further along the ridge, another large rock outcrop – known appropriately as the Black Thumb – rears above the forest. This one is beyond a scramble and surmounting it will demand the skills and equipment of a rock climber.

You might hear kaka during your walk, a bird that symbolises the hopes of a local group called the Bream Head Conservation Trust. The trust is a partnership between local iwi, the community, the Whangarei District Council and DOC. They plan to eliminate pests in the Bream Head Scenic Reserve, and thereby encourage kaka from the nearby Hen and Chickens Islands to once again start breeding on the Northland mainland.

Beyond Black Thumb, a gradual descent through lush bush leads down to open forest with grassy clearings. Here, one branch of the Peach Cove Track drops down to Ocean Beach Road. Carry on the main Te Whara Track for another 15 minutes to reach the second Peach Cove Track junction. Here, the Peach Cove Track leaves the main trail and descends steeply through coastal forest for 200 metres to Peach Cove Hut. Puriri, nikau and pohutukawa are prominent.

Shortly before reaching the hut, the track passes a large pohutukawa growing atop a gigantic boulder. Originally built by the Whangarei Tramping Club, Peach Cove Hut was taken over by DOC in 2002, and subsequently renovated. Occupying a small clearing in the forest, it's tidy and functional, with a water tank and deck. Camping spots exist nearby.

A short five-minute track leads down to Peach Cove itself. The sandy, boulder-fringed beach makes a good place to watch Australasian gannets, variable oystercatchers, red-billed gulls and spotted shags. While often a tranquil place to swim, during easterly gales the sea can become quite rough.

After a night at Peach Cove Hut, head back up the track to the main Te Whara Track. Here, an undulating climb towards Mt Lion ensues, with the track passing more rock pinnacles en route. Unfortunately, the vegetation somewhat restricts the views from Mt Lion (395 m), but after a steepish descent down towards Urquharts Bay, the canopy opens enough to reveal Smugglers Bay at one point. The track can be quite slippery after rain, and rather hard on your knees.

The track emerges onto farmland past a stile, and soon intercepts the Smugglers Bay Track. Head right for 10 minutes to reach Urquharts Bay and the roadend. Energetic trampers, however, might choose instead to complete the enjoyable circuit around Smugglers Bay, Busby Head and the old gun emplacements below Home Point. In times past, Ngatiwai occupied several sites in the area, including a large defensive pa on Home Point. The slopes of Home Point show evidence of house terraces and food storage pits, and Smugglers Bay is an almost continuous midden; all part of a rich history that adds much to the tramp.

Karekare–Whatipu

Duration 1–2 days

Grade Easy–Medium

Times Karekare to Zion Hill Track: 20–25 minutes. Zion Hill Track to Pararaha Stream Track junction: 40–60 minutes. Pararaha Stream Track junction to Pararaha camping area: 20 minutes. Camping area to Gibbons Track: 25–30 minutes. Gibbons Track to Whatipu: 1–1.5 hours. Whatipu to Pararaha Stream via coast: 1.5–2 hours. Pararaha Stream to Karekare: 1–1.5 hours.

Map Q11 Waitakere

Access From the Auckland suburb of Titirangi, follow Scenic Drive for 10 km before turning left onto Piha Road. Follow this for 11 km, then turn left onto Karekare Road. A further 3 km takes you down to the roadend, where there is a carpark, picnic area and toilets.

Alternative Route To shorten the trip considerably, you could simply walk as far as the Pararaha Stream, then head down to the coast and north to Karekare, thereby missing out the southern section to Whatipu.

Information Auckland Regional Council, Arataki Visitor Centre, Ph 09 817 0077, www.arc.govt.nz

This coastal walk is arguably one of the best overnight tramps in the Waitakere Ranges, the densely forested hills on Auckland's northwestern flank. It's a tramp through subtropical forest to a pleasant campsite beside the gorged Pararaha Stream, beyond to the ironsand and bold headlands of Whatipu, and then a coastal stroll back to Karekare. Although the trip can be completed quite comfortably in a longish day, many will want to take a tent and spread it out over a more leisurely weekend. The route lies within the Waitakere Ranges Regional Park, which is administered by the Auckland Regional Council.

The tramp begins at Karekare, a small beach community. From the carpark take the Pohutukawa Glade Walk to a picnic area. Here, a signpost indicates the start of the Zion Hill Track, which follows the route of an old Maori trail to Pararaha. A steady climb ensues up this track onto a forested spur, with some good views back over Karekare Beach and to the distinctive shape of The Watchman – a headland invariably rendered hazy by sea spray. The track is quite muddy in places, and passes through forest

Pararaha River, Waitakere Ranges

dominated by pohutukawa, puriri, manuka and kawakawa. After about 20–25 minutes, you'll reach Mt Zion (272 m) and the junction where the Zion Ridge Track branches off. Stay on the Zion Hill Track. Nikau palms, rimu, tree ferns and the occasional kauri begin to make appearances, as the track traverses an undulating ridge. After crossing a small stream, you enter a kauri grove with some sizeable trees.

The Waitakere Ranges were once covered in mature kauri forest but, not surprisingly, the demands of a growing Auckland soon meant most of it was felled. Later, farming was attempted over much of the Waitakere Ranges, but the region has since largely been left to regenerate.

The track, now increasingly rutted and muddy, crosses a second stream to join the Buck Taylor Track. Head right here, where the track drops down to a coastal wetland in the Pararaha Valley. A signpost at a track junction in the valley indicates the way to a campsite upstream. The Pararaha Stream can be sizeable in flood, and in such conditions can be difficult to cross. The walk from the junction to the campsite takes about 20 minutes. There's a shelter here amongst several grassy camping spots, with the Pararaha Stream gurgling nearby and a pyramid-shaped peak of black volcanic rock prominent beyond. It's a tranquil spot, and hard to imagine a barrage of kauri logs being flushed down-river to feed the Pararaha mill, as occurred in the 1870s. The valley is lined with nikau palms, mahoe and cabbage trees, but unfortunately a growing number of weeds – including inkweed, lily, wandering willy and mist flower – pose problems on the forest floor in this warm, moist climate.

From the camp, the Muir Track climbs steadily onto a ridge, where it joins the Gibbons Track. En route, there's a good viewpoint over the mosaic of small lagoons and wetland vegetation on the beach north of Whatipu. From the viewpoint, the track descends for some distance, finally emerging at Whatipu Stream, where there is a footbridge.

As a side trip, it's possible to follow a rough unmarked route that heads northwards before you cross the footbridge. This leads to some sea caves that were once used as shelter by Maori and, later, as a ballroom for timber workers in the 1920s. There's another campsite here, with a toilet. Beyond the caves, the track peters out. A 4WD track marked on the map is actually the line of the old Karekare–Whatipu tramway, dating back to the days of timber extraction, but this passes through swampland and the coast now makes a better route to Karekare.

Back at the footbridge over the Whatipu Stream, head towards the coast, past the commercial Whatipu campground (which is accessible by road). Beyond the campground, a track leads onto the ironsand of the beach, where you get a good vista of the wild coastline at the northern entrance of Manukau Harbour. Cutter Rock pokes up defiantly, with the impressive Paratutae Island and Ninepin Rock nearby. One of New Zealand's most famous and disastrous shipwrecks occurred here in 1863, when HMS *Orpheus* ran aground on the Manukau sandbar at the cost of 189 lives.

From Whatipu, you begin a coastal walk back to Karekare over the black sands so characteristic of Auckland's western coastline. Amazingly, as little as 100 years ago, the beach here was just a narrow strip between sea and cliffs, not the expansive and still-expanding two-kilometres-wide stretch of today. It's likely that this sand accumulated after being shifted from deposits on the Manukau bar.

Walking in a wild coastal environment is something of a rarity in the North Island, and this is a shoreline to savour. There's the often boisterous Tasman Sea pounding waves onto the sand, a haze of sea spray, the circling of gulls and, inland, the ever-present, brooding, forested cliffs of the Waitakere Ranges. Dotterels and oystercatchers scurry away from you in a cartoon-like flurry of legs, and you may even decide to follow suit, shedding your boots to let the soles of your feet enjoy a sand massage.

Past Pararaha Point, head inland towards Tunnel Point through some large sand dunes to join the trail leading towards Karekare. At Tunnel Point there's another campsite overhung by large pohutukawa, making it a very nice lunch spot. There's also an old rusting steam boiler, once part of the mill operation at Pararaha, from where timber was transported out to Whatipu on the narrow-gauge tramline that hugged coastal cliffs. When the Pararaha mill burnt down in 1881, much of

Nikau palm in flower, Pararaha Valley, Waitakere Ranges

the machinery was shifted to a new mill built at Karekare, but the steam boiler rolled off the rails and was subsequently abandoned.

After walking through the tunnel you emerge on the beach again at Cowan Bay, where the spectacular cliffs of Cowan Point meet the Tasman Sea. Rock platforms just before Karekare Point that used to be dangerous at high tide are now sand-covered and the route is accessible in all but the stormiest and highest spring tides.

Paratahi Island lies just off the coast (although encroaching sand is threatening its status as an island), and there are some interesting rock pools along the shore. At this point you'll probably be sharing the beach with fishers, families, picnickers and those out to enjoy the sea air. Once you round Karekare Point, The Watchman comes into view again, and then it's simply a short stroll inland to the carpark.

Coastline and Paratahi Island, Karekare Beach, Waitakere Ranges Regional Park

Mt Hobson/Hirakimata

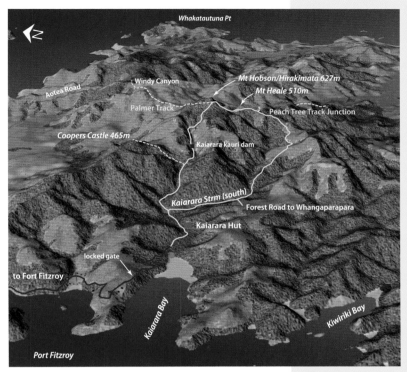

Duration 1–2 days

Grade Medium

Times Roadend to Kaiarara Hut (28 bunks, woodstove, $15/night): 20–30 minutes. Kaiarara to Mt Hobson: 3–4 hours via Kaiarara kauri dam. Mt Hobson to Kaiarara Hut via South Fork Track: 2–3 hours. Note that during heavy rain the streams flood rapidly and this can make the trip impossible.

Map S08

Access From Auckland catch a ferry to Port Fitzroy, from where it's a 3-km walk along Kaiarara Bay Road to the locked gate (consider taking a mountain bike on the ferry, which can be ridden as far as Kaiarara Hut). Alternatively you can fly from Auckland or Waiheke to Great Barrier Island, but will need a taxi or hire car to reach Port Fitzroy.

Alternative Routes From Port Fitzroy, you could also use the Coopers Castle route to access the Kaiarara Dam and Mt Hobson. Past Mt Hobson it is possible to take the Palmers Track to Windy Canyon and exit onto Aotea Road (3 hours). Although shorter, this latter route requires some transport juggling.

Information DOC Great Barrier Area Office, Ph 09 429 0044; DOC Auckland Visitor Centre, Ph 09 379 6476; Great Barrier Infomation Centre, Ph 0800 AUCKLAND (www.greatbarriernz.com)

Great Barrier, the largest island in the Hauraki Gulf and, indeed, the largest off the North Island's coast, is a bush-clad paradise for holidaymakers, surfers and trampers. While getting there presents a bit of a logistical exercise even for Auckland trampers, the island offers this enjoyable overnight walk with a bit of everything: a snatch of coastline, an impressive historic kauri dam, excellent birdlife, distinctive volcanic topography and some fine regenerating kauri forest. The tramp also includes the island's only hut and crosses its highest point, Mt Hobson/Hirakimata, with unsurpassed views over the Hauraki Gulf.

There's a locked gate part of the way down Kaiarara Bay Road, restricting access beyond to those on foot or mountain bike. From here, follow the Forest Road to the Kaiarara Stream. The track is now of 4WD width (it's an old New Zealand Forest Service logging road) and crosses Kaiarara Stream three times before reaching Kaiarara Hut. The hut is among tall stands of manuka and offers bunk space for 28; there are also plenty of camping spots nearby.

View over Port Fitzroy and Little Barrier Island from Mt Hobson

Just up-valley from the hut, the track forks at a signpost at the Kaiarara Track junction. Here, take the left branch; the right follows the Forest Road to Whanga-parapara (a route now popular with mountain bikers). Soon afterward, the track lapses to normal tramping width, crossing through quite lush forest that includes regenerating kauri, nikau palms and the occasional rimu. After rain, the clay soils can be quite greasy and it pays to watch your step. Head straight on at the next track junction (the right branch leads to the south fork of the Kaiarara Stream, along which you'll return from Mt Hobson). The track climbs gradually, crossing the north fork stream a number of times, up to a signposted junction where the Coopers Castle route branches off. Take the right fork. Further along, you reach a signposted side trip to the Kaiarara kauri dam, one of the tramp's highlights.

The Kauri Timber Company, which also built another two dams further upstream, constructed the Kaiarara kauri dam in 1926. Kauri logs were skidded into the stream bed, after which all three dams would be 'tripped', combining to create a flood that swept the logs down to Kaiarara Bay. From there, the logs were rafted to Auckland. Such was the efficiency of kauri loggers in the Kaiarara (altogether, some 27 million metres of timber were extracted from Great Barrier Island) that operations ceased just three years later, in 1929. This lower dam is the best remaining one in New Zealand and stands as a tribute to enormous industry, destructiveness and ingenuity. DOC completed preservation work on the dam in 2000 and plans ongoing maintenance of this historic site.

Back on the main track, you sidle up-valley, crossing numerous footbridges over small watercourses. The remains of a much less impressive kauri dam are passed at one of these streams. Beyond, clear views open up through the forest of the stark volcanic cliffs on the far side of the valley, an indication that the topography is becoming increasingly rugged. Wooden stairs mark the start of some serious climbing, and these lead right to the summit of Mt Hobson. Shortly before the summit, you pass the signposted junction to the Kaiarara south fork and another to Windy Canyon (an alternative way to finish the tramp).

From the trig station on top of Mt Hobson (627 m) there are superlative views over Port Fitzroy, Kaiarara Bay, Whangapoua Beach and Kaitoke, as well as further afield to Cuvier Island, the tip of the Coromandel Peninsula, Little Barrier Island, the Hen and Chickens, Mokohinau and the Poor Knights Islands. This is undoubtedly one of the most extensive views of the Hauraki Gulf, and on a good day it's certainly a place to linger long.

After enjoying the views, take a look at the surrounding forest and several things will become apparent. First, the kauri and other trees on this summit comprise one of the few areas of virgin forest on the island. Second, the flora has an almost subalpine feel to it, with *Dracophyllum*, celery pine, *Quintinia*, mountain flax and yellow-silver pine. One reason DOC has constructed the boardwalk and stairs on the upper slopes of the mountain is to keep trampers off this fragile environment, where a number of rare plants exist; the other is to protect the burrows of black petrels (*Procellaria parkinsoni*), which nest on the summit between October and June. Some 2500 pairs roost on the island, which together with Little Barrier Island is their only remaining breeding ground.

From the summit, go back to the last track junction where the signpost indicates the way to the Kaiarara south fork. Initially the track comprises wooden stairs, but it soon lapses into a normal tramping route – steepish, rocky and rooty. At first it passes through the mature forest that cloaks the summit, but by the time you've reached the base of the spire-shaped Mt Heale, you're in a zone of regenerating manuka, kanuka, towai and five-finger. About 30 minutes from the summit you meet the Peach Tree Track junction – bear right here, following the sign to Kaiarara Hut.

This track follows the stream for a short distance, then sidles along a greasy spur to reach a swingbridge. More gentle sidling across bush faces follows, until the

Mature kauri forest, Mt Hobson

track descends onto a spur that leads down to a fork in the South Kaiarara Stream. Cross here and follow the track downstream to the remains of another kauri dam – this one has only a few flat boards and one main cill log remaining. By now the forest is, once again, subtropical, with nikau palms, kohekohe, puriri and taraire forming a luxuriant, handsome canopy.

Despite the destruction caused by kauri logging and burning, vigorously regenerating forest now covers most of Great Barrier. The island is also lucky enough to be devoid of both possums and mustelids. Although wild cats present a predator problem, the birdlife is extremely good, and it's an unlucky tramper who has not heard several kaka and kakariki by now.

A couple of hundred metres downstream is yet another track junction. The right fork follows the Kaiarara south fork link to the Kaiarara Track, while the left leads through to the Forest Road. Either way takes you back to Kaiarara Hut.

Pinnacles Hut & Kauaeranga Kauri Trail

Duration 1–2 days

Grade Easy

Times Roadend to Hydro Camp via Webb Creek: 1.5-2 hours. Hydro Camp to Pinnacles Hut (80 bunks, gas cooking rings, woodstove, $15/night): 40–60 minutes each way. Climb to The Pinnacles: 1.5-2 hours return. Hydro Camp to roadend via Billy Goat Basin: 2-3 hours. Hut tickets must be purchased well in advance from the Kauaeranga Visitor Centre.

Maps T12 Thames, Coromandel Parkmap

Access Turn off SH 25 onto the Kauaeranga Valley Road 2 km south of Thames. After 13 km the winding road passes an excellent DOC visitor centre (open 8 a.m. to 4 p.m. daily), which has good information on the valley's history and conservation values. The road continues for a further 8 km, past several campgrounds and picnic areas, to the roadend at the Trestle View Campground, where there are toilets.

Information DOC Kauaeranga Visitor Centre, Ph 07 867 9080

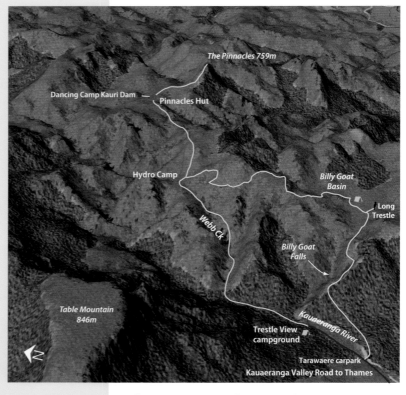

The Kauaeranga Valley near Thames remains one of Coromandel's best-known walking destinations, and in recent years DOC has done much to improve tracks in the area. The best overnight tramp in the park is the increasingly popular Kauaeranga Kauri Trail to Pinnacles Hut – the largest hut in the country with 80 bunks. It's a tramp that offers a snapshot experience of the Coromandel Range, with its regenerating kauri forests, volcanic topography and interesting history.

Between the 1870s and the 1920s the Kauaeranga Valley was a hub of activity, with a large community of people engaged in extracting kauri. From the 1870s the easier slopes were extensively felled, until in the 1890s something of a slump in the kauri industry saw a temporary halt to the logging. By 1912 activity had resumed, but only the more inaccessible trees remained. Tramways and tracks were cut in the bush, but World War I interrupted progress. By the 1920s, bushmen were making a last determined effort to strip the remaining kauri from the upper valley. Dozens of dams were constructed in the headwaters to flush out the logs in destructive floods. Adjacent dams were often 'tripped' at the same time, rushing thousands of logs down to the flats where they could be hauled away for milling. The boom of logs tumbling down in a flood of water could sometimes be heard from as far away as Thames, 18 kilometres distant. The operation was so successful that by 1928 virtually all of the millable kauri was gone, and logging ceased.

In the early 1990s DOC began upgrading some of the historic tracks to form the Kauaeranga Kauri Trail. From the roadend near the Trestle View campground in the Kauaeranga Valley, the well-graded track crosses the Kauaeranga River on a swingbridge, then climbs through regenerating kauri forest beside Webb Creek. An enormous amount of effort has gone into upgrading this section of the track, and it is now a far cry from the muddy, rutted route that existed prior to the 1990s. En route there are some attractive falls, and a few footbridges. After about two hours, the track reaches the Hydro Camp, which was used as a base for workers erecting powerlines over the range in the 1940s. From here take the signposted route towards Pinnacles Hut.

The tramp to the hut passes through more regenerating kauri forest, eventually cresting the broad tops of the Coromandel Range. The hut (built in 1995) has solar lighting, gas cookers and a resident warden. After getting settled into the hut, take the short side track which leads to Dancing Camp Dam (built in 1924), the second largest of the kauri dams that were constructed in the valley. The camp was so named because bushmen from various camps met there to dance on occasions. Men often had to make do dancing with each other before they got a turn with one of the few women present in the camp. During

Pinnacles Hut, Coromandel Forest Park

1994, DOC archaeologists partially restored the dam, using kauri logs that were washed out during an exceptionally heavy flood the year before.

There are formed camping sites near the Dancing Camp Dam for trampers who are carrying a tent. Another popular side trip from the hut is the steep climb up to The Pinnacles (759 m). DOC extensively upgraded this track in 2007, but trampers should be aware that it is still steeper than the rest of the Kauaeranga Kauri Trail, with ladders and grab rungs on some sections. However, once on top your effort is rewarded by a superb panorama over the surrounding range, with the ocean visible off both sides of the Coromandel Peninsula.

From Pinnacles Hut, return to the Hydro Camp. Here the Kauaeranga Kauri Trail climbs and sidles along to Billygoat Basin, reaching a viewpoint over the valley at one point. A series of stone steps leads down to a crossing of Billy Goat Creek, and shortly beyond to a small clearing where there is a basic campsite and a toilet. Nearby is a short side track to a viewpoint of the (now collapsed) Long Trestle, a 160-metre-long bridge that was part of a tramline built in the 1920s. Shortly beyond here, head right at a track junction (left leads to the Tarawaere Dam).

More sidling leads to a good viewpoint over the 180-metre Billygoat Falls – a site where many kauri logs were wastefully smashed to matchsticks over a huge drop when loggers attempted to flush them into the valley below during the 1880s. Beyond the viewpoint the track drops sharply down what was called the 'Billygoat Incline' – part of the 1920s tramline built to circumvent the destructive falls. Here steam haulers lowered logs into the Kauaeranga Valley down slopes that approached 45 degrees at their steepest. DOC has restored a section of the original incline on part of the track.

Lower down, the trail reaches gentler gradients, and finally crosses a swingbridge over the Kauaeranga River to end at the Tarawaere carpark. The main track start is just 300 metres back up the road, at the Trestle View Campground.

Dancing Camp Dam pictured shortly after its 1994 restoration

Leitch's Clearing & Hut

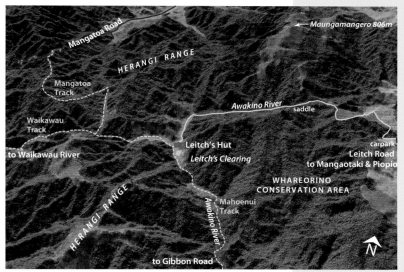

Duration 1–2 days

Grade Easy–Medium

Times Leitch Road to Leitch's Hut (16 bunks, woodstove, $5/night) via Leitch's Track: 3 hours

Map R17 Awakino

Access From SH3, turn off at Piopio onto Mangaotaki Road. Follow this for 16 km to Mangaotaki, then turn off onto Leitch Road and drive 5 km to the carpark.

Alternative Routes There are several other options for reaching Leitch's Hut, which include starting from the Waikawau River (Waikawau Track, 7–8 hours), Gibbon Road (Mahoenui Track, 3–4 hours), and the Mangatoa Road (Mangatoa Track, 4–5 hours). All of these are medium-grade routes. Note that the tracks to Pomorangi Road from Leitch's Clearing and the Mangatoa Track have been closed.

Information DOC Maniapoto Area Office, Ph 07 878 1050

Leitch's Hut, built by DOC in 1994, is testimony to the power of a hut in attracting people. It lies in a grassy clearing roughly at the centre of the King Country's Whareorino Conservation Area, a locale that received little attention from anyone other than the odd hunter prior to the hut's construction. A tramp into Leitch's Hut is a fairly gentle affair, suitable for families with school-aged children, and once there, you have the chance of seeing long-tailed bats, New Zealand falcons and bellbirds.

The track to Leitch's Hut follows an old route, intended for a road that was never built. From a signposted carpark on Leitch Road, it climbs steadily beside a fenceline before plunging into regenerating bush. Clay soils, where exposed, can be slippery after rain, but after about an hour you reach a low, forested saddle and the boundary of the Whareorino Conservation Area. From the saddle, a well-benched trail wends its way down into the headwaters of the Awakino River, with occasional glimpses of the surrounding ridges. There are tree ferns galore, often effectively shading your view of the higher forest above, which is dominated by tawa, rata and hinau. The track finally emerges onto the northern arm of Leitch's Clearing, where there is a gate, signpost and track junction.

Head left here, following grassy flats before sidling around an attractive bend in the Awakino River. Shortly afterwards you'll come to the central part of the clearing and the spacious hut. Leitch's Hut can be popular at weekends, but for those with tents there's plenty of space to camp. From the hut's veranda views open to steep bluffs on the nearby Herangi Range, which boasts a number of subalpine plants, including bog-cushion plants and pahautea, neither of which are found elsewhere in the King Country. Its other distinction is the presence of native Archey's frogs, a surprise discovery in the early 1990s, as their nearest relatives live in the Coromandel, some 250 kilometres distant. Recently, these endangered frogs have become even further threatened by the *Chytrid* fungus, and to prevent its further spread, DOC have closed off the entire northern part of the Conservation Area, including Pomorangi Track and the route along the Herangi Range from the Mangatoa Track. During the evening, you may like to watch out for long-tailed bats flitting around, catching insects even more deftly than welcome swallows.

Surrounding macrocarpa trees provide shelter for the hut from breezes that sweep through the clearing. These trees were the work of pioneer farmer Sam Leitch, who lived here for 20 years, in a whare he built himself.

Leitch was one of the first surveyors to visit Whareorino, in 1902, and believing it would become valuable property he subsequently bought land around the clearing that now bears his name. It was supposed to become the hub of a busy crossroads, connecting routes from the inland towns of Mangaotaki and Mahoenui, to Waikawau on the west coast. Once Leitch had bought the land, he planted the macrocarpas and an eleagnus hedge, built his whare and cut bush to make the clearing. This accomplished, he drove sheep up the Awakino River to farm. Over the next 20 years the pioneer farmer toiled to extend the clearing, leading a solitary life before becoming disillusioned when the roads never came, and finally leaving. His whare succumbed to the elements in the 1950s.

During the morning, you can make a couple of side trips in the western and south-

Leitch's Hut at dusk, Leitch's Clearing, Awakino Valley

eastern branches of the clearing, part of the way along the Mangatoa or Mahoenui tracks respectively. Either of these can make a through trip, although both will require pre-arranged transport. Most parties return the same way they came in.

No doubt Sam Leitch would approve of the hut, knowing that his clearing has finally become a destination, albeit for trampers, not vehicles.

Leitch's Clearing and the Awakino River

Pirongia Mountain

Duration 1–2 days

Grade Medium

Times Grey Road end to Tirohanga Track: 1–1.5 hours. Tirohanga Track to Pirongia summit: 2–3 hours. Summit to Pahautea Hut (6 bunks, no fireplace, $5/night): 20 minutes. Pahautea Hut to Grey Road end via Mahaukura Track: 4–5 hours.

Map S15 Te Awamutu

Access From Pirongia township, drive north for 5 km, and turn left onto Bridge Road. After 1 km turn left onto Hodgson Road, and finally left again onto Grey Road. At the roadend, there are toilets, a carpark, an information shelter and the Pirongia Forest Park Lodge.

Alternative Routes Corcoran Road provides quicker access to Pahautea Hut for trampers who don't want to complete the round trip from Grey Road. DOC, in partnership with the Te Araroa Trust, are also developing a track (called the Hihikiwi Track) to Hihikiwi from Pirongia West Road, which will provide an excellent alternative route to Pahautea Hut.

Information DOC Waikato Area Office, Ph 07 838 3363

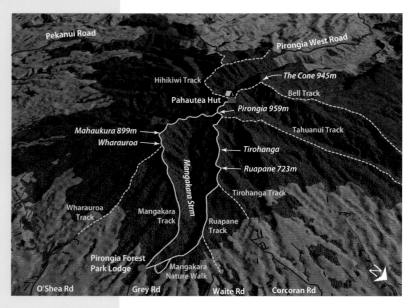

Pirongia's distinctive green summit dominates the skyline south of Hamilton. Although it no longer resembles one, the forest-clad mountain was once a large volcano. Since volcanic activity ceased some 1.5 million years ago, the erosive forces of wind, frost and water have whittled the mountain to its present shape, but from some viewpoints it is still possible to see the rough outline of where the main crater once existed.

Pirongia (959 m) is probably the most sought-after summit in the Waikato, and the views from the top alone make the effort to reach it worthwhile. The easiest access is via the Tirohanga Track, starting at Corcoran Road. However, those seeking a slightly more rugged round trip can start instead from Grey Road, taking a link track onto the Tirohanga Track and returning over the Mahaukura Track. It pays to carry plenty of water, as there's precious little between the Mangakara Stream and Pahautea Hut.

From the Grey Road carpark, head towards the Mangakara Nature Walk, a well-benched and gravelled track popular with families. Here, rimu and kahikatea dominate tawa, kohekohe and nikau palms. Pirongia is interesting botanically, because it marks a transition from the warmth-loving kauri forests of the north to the beech and podocarp-beech forests of the south. The park's latitude marks the naturally occurring southern limit for such species as kauri and mangeao.

After crossing the Mangakara Stream via a footbridge, turn left and follow a sign-posted trail that connects with the Ruapane Track. The junction with the Ruapane Track is reached shortly afterward, where you bear left (the right branch goes to Waite Road).

Some 60 to 90 minutes after leaving the carpark, you reach the main Tirohanga Track. A short, steep climb ensues to the summit of Ruapane, a rocky knoll with extensive views northward over the Waikato lowlands. From here, the track becomes narrower, climbing over or around a series of spectacular tors, some cloaked in rata and kamahi forest. The rugged nature of this ridge is better understood when you realise that it was once the lip of Pirongia's volcanic crater.

The delicate volcanic soils are very prone to becoming muddy after rain, but in recent years boardwalks have been built to avoid the worst of Pirongia's once-notorious mud. On the summit of Pirongia there's a modern viewing platform which you can climb to gain views over the stunted forest. Panoramic views of the Waikato, and of Raglan and Kawhia harbours unfold before you. However in the wrong weather, Pirongia's summit can be a bleak place.

Beyond the summit, the track leads down through pahautea (mountain cedar), Hall's

Sunrise over Waikato basin from Pirongia, Waikato

totara and kamahi forest to Pahautea Hut. Botanically, this area is of interest not only because of the pahautea but also for the presence of the root parasite *Dactylanthus taylori*. You may see some of the latter covered in wire cages, the result of the concerted effort DOC is making to protect these plants from the ravages of possums.

Tirohanga, Pirongia Forest Park

Pahautea Hut gets considerable use, and during summer it may pay to carry a tent. There are six formed campsites nearby, and a cooking shelter is attached to the hut. Te Araroa, the national trail connecting Cape Reinga with Bluff, now traverses Pirongia Forest Park. The Te Araroa Trust, in partnership with DOC, plans to install 800 metres of boardwalk between Pahautea Hut and the nearby summit of Hihikiwi, which will make it one of the longest boardwalked sections of track in New Zealand. Once complete, this will make an outstanding side trip from the hut, and trampers will be able to admire the sunset (or sunrise) over Pirongia from a viewing platform at Hihikiwi.

Before departing the hut in the morning, fill your water bottle from the hut water tank. Head back up to the summit and take the signposted track along the Mahaukura Track. This route is more difficult than the Tirohanga Track, but is equally rewarding and has some excellent viewpoints. There's a considerable amount of up and down involved, plus some scrambling and a few sections of steps. When its leaves are new, the spindly spiderwood, *Dracophyllum latifolium*, gives the forest a dash of red.

Mahaukura and Wharauroa are both prominent rocky knolls, offering clear views over the Waikato, the King Country and the town of Te Awamutu. At the summit of Wharauroa, a chain helps you to secure yourself around a sloping rocky section. Past the junction with the Wharauroa Route (which leads to O'Shea Road), the track passes through tawa forest at a more leisurely gradient on one of the most pleasant ridges in the park. The tramp ends back at the Grey Road carpark.

Waitawheta Valley

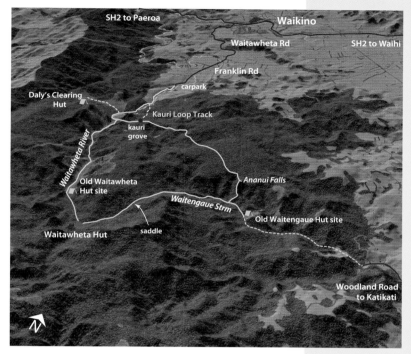

Duration 2 days

Grade Easy–Medium

Times Franklin Road end to Waitawheta Hut (26 bunks, serviced, $15/night, hut warden present during summer): 3.5–4 hours. Waitawheta Hut to Waitengaue River: 2–3 hours. Waitengaue River to Kauri Loop Track: 3–4 hours. Kauri Loop Track to Franklin Road: 1–1.5 hours.

Maps T13 Paeroa, Kaimai-Mamaku Forest Park Map

Access From SH2 (which runs through the Karangahake Gorge), take Waitawheta Road, turn into Spence Road and then turn immediately into Franklin Road; where there is a carpark about 500 metres from the roadend.

Information DOC Tauranga Area Office, Ph 07 578 7677

The Waitawheta River drains the heart of the Kaimai Range, where several tracks provide opportunities for a range of weekend-length trips. Perhaps the best is a varied two-day tramp in the Waitawheta Valley, which starts near the Karangahake Gorge. The route features a modern comfortable hut, some impressive kauri trees and an interesting history. During summer, trampers can find plenty of swimming holes for splashing around in the sizeable Waitawheta River.

From Franklin Road, a good track leads over farmland for 25 minutes up the Waitawheta Valley, passing through patches of regenerating forest. A gate marks the entrance to the forest park. Pass a track that branches off to the Kauri Loop Track and another that branches off to Daly's Clearing and hut. The main valley track passes one small waterfall, surrounded by an attractive bank of parataniwha. By now it will be obvious that the Waitawheta Valley track follows the route of an old kauri-milling tramline, progressing at a very gentle gradient. In many places the original sleepers are exposed, still in place, and sections of old rail have also been unearthed by recent DOC excavations.

After a further hour you pass the second branch of the Kauri Loop Track (where you'll finish). The track crosses the Waitawheta River six times; the first ford was bridged in 2007, and DOC also plans to build bridges over the third and fourth fords, leaving just three unbridged. Needless to say, the unbridged fords should not be attempted when the river is flooded. Concrete pilings, the sole remains of tramway bridges that used to span the river in the kauri-logging era, remain at some of these crossings, and in one place DOC has restored an old rail bogey, complete with a log on top.

Just past the sixth river crossing, you reach a grassy clearing, where the old Waitawheta Hut was sited, with a composting toilet and ample camping spots. A further 30-minute tramp leads to the new Waitawheta Hut, built in 2004 on the site of the cookhouse of an historic kauri mill and bush camp. In the 1990s this was an overgrown, gorse-studded spot with only a few bogey wheels to interest trampers. Since then, however, DOC and volunteer groups have excavated a number of interesting artefacts, and erected good information panels explaining the history.

Gorge in the Waitawheta valley, Kaimai-Mamaku Forest Park

The Waitawheta Valley was first logged around 1900, with a lot of the timber being used by the Waihi Mining Company. Later, the Kauri Timber Company extracted kauri, floating logs down to the tramline, where horses pulled the timber out to Owharoa. In 1923 the Kauri Timber Company lost the logging rights, which went to a shrewd entrepreneur named Bob Joughan. He extended the tramline up the valley, and built a new sawmill (near the new hut site). By converting a Fordson tractor for use on the tramway, he eliminated the need for horses, and made more efficient use of each kauri by cutting the tree as low as possible, and also using the crown. Loggers fed the mill by hauling logs down from kauri groves on the faces and ridge above. More kauri was floated down the valley from upstream dams, and arrested at nearby timber booms. All the logs were milled on site, and green timber taken down the valley. Kauri logging continued only for another four years, ending in 1927, by which time Joughan was a wealthy man.

It is well worth spending an afternoon or morning exploring the area around the hut. One 25-minute figure 8 trail leads around the recently-excavated mill site and timber booms. Another 50-minute bush walk loops around a forested face behind the hut. Even the new hut itself sports a huge vertical saw blade, once used on the site.

Back across the footbridge over the Waitawheta River, head up-valley for five minutes until a signposted track branches off to the left. This leads eastwards over a low saddle into the Waitengaue Valley, reached after 2–3 hours. Once in the Waitengaue Valley, the track crosses the river to a signposted track junction.

Unless you want to camp the night or tramp to Woodland Road (an alternative finish) take the Ananui Falls track (the downstream track reaches a camping area after 15 minutes, site of the old Waitengaue Hut which burnt down in 2002).

From the junction, the Ananui Falls track climbs sharply up a ridge for 20–30 minutes until you first hear the falls. Here, on a small knoll, an unmarked side track leads for two minutes to a viewpoint of the slender 106-metre falls. The main track climbs gradually for 20–30 more minutes, reaching a signpost indicating a short side trip to the top of the waterfall. (Near the junction are a couple of flats suitable for camping in the forest.) In a setting among some substantial kauri, some more than a metre in diameter, the top of the falls provides quite a giddy viewpoint down into the valley below – but take care not to get too close to the edge.

Back on the main track you climb gradually to a flat forested plateau, where patches of gorse indicate past logging activity. Although well marked, this section can be overgrown, so take care not to divert off onto an old road. After some tiresome trudging up a sloping ridge, the track eventually begins to descend to the Kauri Loop Track.

Here two massive kauri trees penetrate the forest canopy; the largest remaining specimens in the park which were fortunately spared from logging due to their inaccessible location. From the kauri grove take the Gully Stream Track which leads steeply down for 30 minutes into the Waitawheta

Kauri tree, Agathis australis

Valley. Here you ford the Waitawheta River to rejoin the main Waitawheta Track again. An easy 60–90 minute stroll completes the circuit to Franklin Road.

Te Rereatukahia Hut

KAIMAI–MAMAKU FOREST PARK

Duration 1–2 days

Grade Easy

Times Tuahu Track to Tuahu Saddle: 2.5–3 hrs. Tuahu Saddle to Te Rereatukahia Hut (16 bunks, category 3): 1.5–2 hours. Te Rereatukahia Hut to roadend: 2 hours.

Maps T14 Morrinsville, Kaimai-Mamaku Forest Park Map

Access From SH 2, turn onto Hot Springs Road 5 km south of Katikati. Follow this road to the end, where there is a carpark and toilet.

Information DOC Tauranga Area Office, Ph 07 578 7677

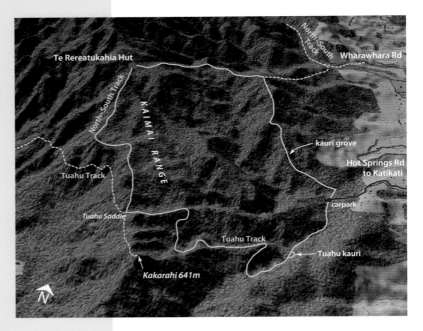

The Kaimai–Mamaku Forest Park runs the length of the Kaimai Range, a spine of mountains with similar volcanic origins to the more northerly Coromandel Range. Although there are no open tops along this walk, the crest of the range does offer good viewpoints. The circuit to Te Rereatukahia Hut can be completed easily in one day or even more leisurely over two. As well as offering good views, the track passes through some of the best remaining kauri forest in the park, here nearing its southern limit.

Even from the Hot Springs Road carpark you can see some sizeable kauri trees, emergent above the surrounding canopy. From here, take the Tuahu Track, and follow it for 20 minutes before reaching a detour to the Tuahu kauri branching off to the left. After a five-minute stroll, this side trail reaches a boardwalk and viewing platform around the magnificent Tuahu kauri, the largest of which has a 2.7-metre diameter trunk that rises 12.8 metres to its first branches.

Past the kauri trees, the track rejoins the main Tuahu Track after another five minutes. Originally a Maori trail that provided access across the Kaimai Range between the Bay of Plenty and the Waikato, the Tuahu Track was reconstructed in the 1890s along a gentler gradient as required by a bridle trail. The track sidles fairly gentle slopes, crosses a stream and then ascends steadily, at one point providing views of Tauranga Harbour.

At Tuahu Saddle, on the crest of the Kaimai Range, the vegetation becomes more stunted, and you reach a four-way track junction. Here, the main Tuahu Track continues westwards, while the North–South Track intersects it. A worthwhile side trip is the 30-minute walk south to the knoll Kakarahi, where there are excellent viewpoints north to Te Aroha and southwards across the rugged slopes of Queen Victoria Head and other craggy peaks. Westwards lie the forested summits of the Waikato's Pirongia and Maungatautari.

Back at the Tuahu Saddle track junction, head north. The track here can be quite muddy and in places skirts an old fenceline. While this is not a particularly interesting section, it's not too long before you reach Te Rereatukahia Hut. The hut has bunk space for 12 people, but no woodstove or fireplace. Scrubby forest and stunted rimu trees surround the small hut clearing, where there is limited camping. As it is fairly close to the roadend, the hut gets a lot of use and can be a bit musty and dark, but it's not an unpleasant place to pass the night.

In the morning you might be roused by the sounds of kereru, silvereyes, fantails, and grey warblers, or by the staccato call of whitehead flocks. From the hut, the track starts off a little boggy, with supplejack hanging overhead, but soon after it dries out somewhat following a gentle descent. A slight rise leads to a broad spur and a track junction. The left branch follows a new section of the re-routed North–South Track. Instead, head right, passing through an attractive stand of tall tawa trees. From a small knoll, the track drops towards Te Rereatukahia Stream, entering a large stand of pole kauri en route. While none of the trees have a diameter of more than a metre, they give a good sense of how

Kauri forest, near Te Rereatukahia Hut

dominant kauri once were in these forests. Several have gum oozing from their trunks, and the ground is covered with the yellow-brown spikes of jettisoned leaves.

Closer to the stream, there's a subtropical feel to the forest, with nikau palms, puriri trees, abundant ferns and occasional columns of mangemange disappearing into the canopy. A flat terrace beside the stream provides a pleasant place for a snack, then it's a hop across stepping-stones to a short uphill climb and the carpark. At the end of the trip, a relaxing soak in hot pools at the nearby Sapphire Springs campground proves well worthwhile.

Fallen kauri leaves, Kaimai–Mamaku Forest Park

Midway Hut, Horomanga Valley

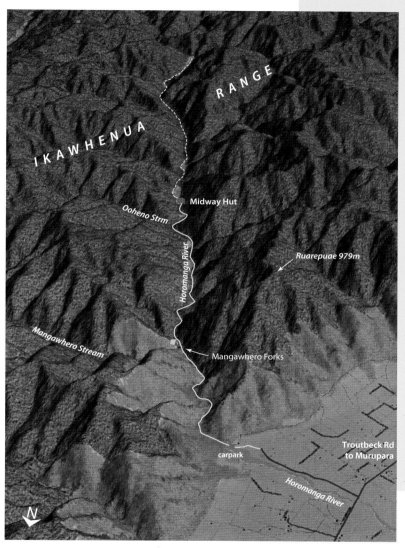

Duration 2 days

Grade Medium

Times Roadend to Mangawhero Forks: 1–1.5 hours. Mangawhero Forks to Midway Hut (9 bunks, wood stove, $5/night): 1.5–2 hours.

Maps V17 Murupara, Urewera Parkmap

Access From SH 38, 2 km south of Murupara, turn off onto Troutbeck Road and follow this for 13 km. Turn right onto an unsignposted gravel road just before the bridge over the Horomanga River. There's a carpark at the end of the road, on a terrace above the river.

Alternative Route From Midway Hut, tracks lead into the headwaters of the Horomanga River, and beyond to Mangapouri and Okui huts

Information DOC Opotiki Area Office, Ph 07 315 1001; email, opotiki-ao@doc.govt.nz

By far the majority of trampers who visit Te Urewera National Park come to enjoy the tracks around Lakes Waikaremoana and Waikareiti. As attractive as these lakes are, they don't embody the essential Te Urewera; that vast extent of broken, complicated terrain threaded by rivers and blanketed by forest. It's the sort of country that children's author

47

Midway Hut, Horomanga Valley

(and ex-deer culler) Jack Lasenby calls 'The Vast Untrodden Urewera' in his excellent Harry Wakatipu novels.

This tramp up the Horomanga Valley gives a good sense of the bush-and-river experience so typical of northern Te Urewera. The Horomanga River filters out of the Ikawhenua Range through a gap in the extensive bush ridges known as the Galatea Faces. It has the added advantage of involving considerably less driving from Auckland, Hamilton or Rotorua than most other parts of the park. Take a fly or tent during summer; mainly because of the hut's popularity with hunters and anglers, but also because there are so many delightful places to camp en route.

From Murupara, the Galatea Faces of Te Urewera rise abruptly and steeply, a marked contrast from the farmed flats surrounding the township. Be warned: tramping to Midway Hut involves some 40 river crossings, and you should not attempt the trip after heavy rain or on a poor forecast. During winter, the river level is generally higher than in summer, but should not present any difficulties when it is running clear. Happily, as the valley runs in a northerly direction, large parts of it remain out of shadow even during the colder months.

From the carpark, the track immediately plunges into the first crossing, one of some 14 required to reach Mangawhero Forks. Steep bush faces rise above the river, and the valley is cloaked in tree species (such as kanuka) that suggest a history of fire. The introduced weed buddleia sprouts quite densely in places, but gets less common further up-valley. Watch out for whio (blue duck).

At Mangawhero Forks, be careful to avoid heading up the side track that branches up the Mangawhero Stream on the true right. A short distance up the Horomanga River, the track passes the site of the old Mangawhero (Red Creek) Hut, now removed. Camping is possible here.

Upstream, the Horomanga remains enclosed by steep valley walls, but by now the forest is virgin, dominated by fine stands of tawa. The well-formed and occasionally marked track follows along terraces for the most part, and crosses the river regularly. Don't be fooled by the map (which shows only a couple of stream crossings): there are at least another 25 before Midway Hut. Happily, almost all of the fords occur where the river is more gravelly than bouldery, although a stout stick or walking pole is recommended to assist your balance.

The valley opens out as you progress, until you reach the first of some delightful grassy river flats. During summer, these make excellent places to camp. The Ooheno Stream, tumbling in on the true right, forms a landmark to gauge your progress. Midway Hut is located about 30 minutes walk upstream. Situated on the true left, up on an old river terrace and surrounded by bush, the hut is of a design peculiar to the Whirinaki–Te Urewera area, with three tiers of three bunks. In addition, Midway has a covered veranda, and an outside fireplace.

A pair of whio (blue duck) on the Horomanga River

Horomanga River, Te Urewera National Park

A pleasant evening can be passed sitting at the veranda table, watching the last of the light play over the forest and ridge beyond. Kahikatea and rimu emerge above the canopy of tawa. Whio often move up or downstream at dusk; listen out for the shrill, distinctive whistle of the male.

While longer trips up into the headwaters of the Horomanga are certainly possible, most trampers will simply head back downstream to their car – this time with the current providing more assistance at the fords. Trampers with more time on their hands could enjoy a short walk to the Te Rereotawhiuau Falls (1 hour return), or the strenuous climb to Maunga Tawhiuau (4–5 hours return), both of which also start from Troutbeck Road.

Lake Waikaremoana

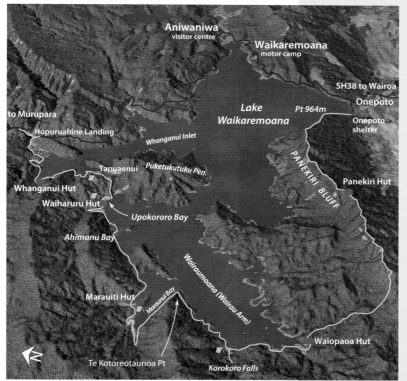

Duration 4–5 days

Grade Medium

Times Onepoto to Pane-kiri Hut (36 bunks, gas heater): 4–6 hours. Panekiri to Waiopaoa Hut (30 bunks, $25/night): 3–4 hours. Waiopaoa to Marauiti Hut (26 bunks, gas heater, $25/night): 4–5 hours. Marauiti to Waiharuru Hut (40 bunks, gas heater, $25/night): 2 hours. Waiharuru to Whanganui Hut (18 bunks, gas heater, $25/night): 2.5 hours. Whanganui to Hopuruahine roadend: 1–1.5 hours. **Note** The tramp is one of the Great Walks, and all huts must be pre-booked with DOC. Respect signposted areas of private land on the lake edge through which the track passes.

Maps W18 Waikaremoana, Te Urewera Parkmap

Access The Aniwaniwa Visitor Centre is located beside SH 38, about 2 hours drive east from Murupara and 1 hours drive west from Wairoa. At the nearby small village of Waikaremoana there's a motorcamp and shop. As each end of the tramp lies at opposite sides of the lake, you'll need to organise transport. Usually the best option is to arrange a water taxi, which departs from the motor camp. DOC can provide details of the service.

Alternative Route Using a water taxi allows you to complete any section of the tramp rather than the whole circuit.

Information DOC Aniwaniwa Area Office, Ph 06 837 3803, urewerainfo@doc.govt.nz; Great Walk bookings, Ph 0800 492 665

Some of the most attractive podocarp-beech forests in the country, a large lake set in the North Island's biggest national park, and an excellent network of huts and campsites make the Lake Waikaremoana circuit a classic tramp. Although the 46-kilometre walk is a bit ambitious over the course of a normal weekend (unless you're feeling particularly energetic), it does make a good option for long weekends. The track is one of the eight Great Walks managed by DOC and, owing to its popularity (especially over summer and Easter), huts must be pre-booked. While this requires some advance planning, it does ensure you have a bunk in the hut.

As the tramp only partially circumnavigates the lake, you must decide which direction to walk in. This description follows the clockwise direction, beginning from Onepoto on the lake's southeastern corner. The track starts a short distance up a side road, passing the Onepoto shelter en route. Although this is a Great Walk, it's far from a gravelled path and is refreshingly back-country in flavour.

Initially, the track climbs steadily, but by no means steeply, through a mix of tawari, kamahi and beech. Quite quickly you gain height to emerge on top of the first viewpoint of the Panekiri Bluff, an impressive rampart overlooking Lake Waikaremoana. The lake spreads in many directions, its long fingers probing west and north, with the forests and crumpled ridges of the northern Te Urewera beyond. There's nowhere else quite like this in the park, or indeed, the whole country.

Dawn over Lake Waikaremoana from Panekiri Hut

Higher up, silver beech dominates and there are the usual forest birds: silvereyes, fantails, grey warblers and whiteheads. By the time you reach Pt 964, most of the climbing is over and the track largely follows the ridge crest, broken by regular viewpoints. Shortly before Panekiri Hut, on a sharp section of the ridge, there's a series of steps to negotiate.

Dawn at Panekiri Hut will hopefully reward you with a vista of the lake, although mist and cloud do often surround the hut and bluffs. If so, you're partially compensated by the fact that the next section of track passes through sublime silver beech forest, made even more enchanting when it's misty. Kaka and kakariki may also be heard as you pass through. The track continues to undulate along the Panekiri Range for some distance before dropping off on a spur towards the lake and Waiopaoa Hut. A new 30-bunk hut has recently been built, replacing the old 22-bunk hut. There's a camping area nearby.

From Waiopaoa Hut the track skirts the shore and changes character accordingly. The surface is more muddy and less sandy than it has been, and kanuka and wheki-ponga become dominant. These pioneer plants are reclaiming ground that was exposed after the lake level was lowered by 5 metres during hydro development in 1946. About an hour beyond Waiopaoa Hut you reach a side trail that leads up to the Korokoro Falls – a diversion well worth the effort. A 20-minute climb beside the Korokorowhaitiri Stream, which is crossed at one point, leads to the falls: an almost perfect cascade tumbling 22 metres over a straight-edged escarpment. The falls generate a fair breeze, and the viewing spot can be quite damp – a situation favoured by the kidney ferns that are prevalent there.

Back on the main track, you cross a large footbridge and pass another camping area (Korokoro), which has – like all those on the circuit – a cooking shelter complete with sinks. From the camp the track begins to sidle around some steeper parts of the lake, often through beech forest. It crosses numerous streams and there are some delightful scenes as you look through the pole beech to the soft blue water beyond. Here, you may spot kingfishers scrutinising the lake.

After the track rounds Te Kotoreotaunoa Point, it makes a long detour up a valley that drains into Maraunui Bay. This proves to be a somewhat frustrating section, as you can see your destination on the opposite bank for some time as you walk away from it.

At Maraunui there's a substantial DOC base, with the Maraunui campsite nearby. Trampers wanting a hut, however, have to cross a small peninsula to Marauiti Bay. Marauiti Hut has perhaps the nicest location of all the lakeside huts, overlooking a rounded forest headland that projects into the lake, which is often clotted with black swans.

Beyond Marauiti Hut, the track climbs over another forested peninsula, passes Te Totara and Ahimanu Bays, then crosses to an inlet at Upokororo Bay. Here lies Waiharuru Hut, with 40 bunks the largest of those on the Great Walk. It's set in a pleasant sunny spot, with a grassy area for camping and views of the Panekiri Range in sharp profile on the opposite side of the lake.

After departing from Waiharuru, the track leaves the Wairaumoana Inlet, the largest of those in the lake. These long arms are actually old river valleys, drowned when the lake was formed. Waikaremoana is a comparatively young lake, created some 2200 years ago when a major landslide from the nearby Ngamoko Range dammed the Waikaretaheke River. That such beauty can come from a colossal moment of destruction seems quite uplifting.

From Waiharuru Hut you cross another large footbridge, then sidle around the shore past the site of the old Te Puna Hut. From here, a significant ascent crosses over a neck of the Puketukutuku Peninsula. Stoat traps housed in wooden boxes lie beside this section of the track, part of a DOC predator control programme on the peninsula aimed at protecting the North Island brown kiwi. Kiwi are present in relatively high numbers in the forests of Te Urewera, and you're likely to hear some at night, especially if you're camping.

There are some charming sections of forest here, which is a mixture of tawa and rimu with the occasional northern rata

Misty dawn at Marauiti Bay, Lake Waikaremoana

and dense areas of Smith's tree fern in the gullies. Over the other side of the peninsula you reach the final camping area, Tapuaenui. From here the track follows the lake once again, brushing the fairly intricate shoreline of the Whanganui Inlet. Patches of kanuka intersperse with beech, and from some points you can see the road on the far side of the inlet. Depending on your mood, this is either an intrusion into your experience or a welcome sign the end is nigh!

Whanganui Hut lies at the head of the inlet and is the smallest and least used of all the huts on the Great Walk. From here, the track meanders around the shore for an hour or so, then crosses the Hopuruahine Stream via a footbridge to reach the road. If you are expecting a ride back in a water taxi, there's a landing en route.

While you might have to share the lake with boaties and increasing numbers of sea kayakers, the walk around Lake Waikaremoana really is a highlight of North Island tramping: the bold views from Panekiri contrast with the more subtle forested shore scenes, while the silent and watchful gaze of lakeside kingfishers contrasts with the harsh calls of kaka deep in the forest. All in all, this Great Walk is really a must at some point in your tramping career.

Marauiti Hut, Lake Waikaremoana

Sandy Bay Hut, Lake Waikareiti

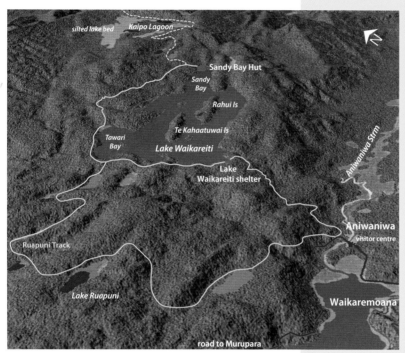

Duration 2 days

Grade Easy

Times Aniwaniwa to Lake Waikareiti shelter: 1 hour. Shelter to Sandy Bay Hut (18 bunks, gas heater, $25/night): 3 hours. (Note that the hut must be booked in advance.)

Maps W18 Waikaremoana, Te Urewera Parkmap

Access The Aniwaniwa Visitor Centre is located beside SH 38; about 2 hours drive east from Murupara and 1 hours drive west from Wairoa. At the nearby small village of Waikaremoana there's a motorcamp and shop. DOC hires out dinghies, stored at the Lake Waikareiti shelter, which can be used to row to Sandy Bay.

Alternative Route The Ruapani Track offers an appealing alternative return route (allow 6 hours from Sandy Bay to Aniwaniwa).

Information DOC Aniwaniwa, Ph 06 837 3803, urewerainfo@doc.govt.nz

Lake Waikareiti is a small, island-studded body of water lying northeast of Lake Waikaremoana. Although both were created by large landslides, Waikareiti is a much older lake (formed some 18,000 years ago) and consequently offers gentler, subtler terrain than its larger neighbour. The walk to the comfortable Sandy Bay Hut at the northern end of Lake Waikareiti is one of the most delightful and relaxing tramps in this book, and makes an ideal destination for families with school-aged children. On a calm day, watching the reflections of the rounded, bush-clad islands reflected in the lake offers one of the most tranquil back-country experiences imaginable.

An excellent option is to walk into Lake Waikareiti shelter, hire a dinghy and row to the hut, exploring some of the islands en route. With a party of four or more, it would be possible to both row and walk on alternate days. Not surprisingly, Sandy Bay is very

55

popular – not only with trampers, but also anglers and hunters – so the hut and dinghies must be pre-booked with DOC.

The Lake Waikareiti track begins just a couple of hundred metres from the Aniwaniwa visitor centre and immediately plunges into dense Te Urewera forest. It's extremely well-benched and graded, climbing slowly around several broad bush faces where many of the shadier spots are lined with fuchsia. Several small streams (all bridged) are crossed before you crest a low saddle just above the lake. Beside the lake edge is a basic day shelter, and nearby are the dinghies and a locked shed (which contains the oars). For those continuing on foot, the track enters the bush again, sidling above the lake at first, then curling inland.

The Te Urewera forests here are a mixture of mainly red and silver beech combined with rimu. Unlike in many other North Island forests, the birdlife is generally abundant, and you're likely to encounter kaka, kakariki, kereru, riflemen, tomtits and robins. At night you may also hear the plaintive calls of North Island brown kiwi.

The track passes the turn-off to the Ruapani Track (an excellent alternative return route), then sidles close to the lake edge once again at Tawari Bay. From here, nearby Te Kahaatuwai Island is clearly visible, but for now its slightly larger neighbour, Rahui Island, remains obscured. The latter is unusual in that it harbours a tiny lakelet.

Lake Waikareiti, Te Urewera National Park

From Tawari Bay, the track climbs a moderate slope, with sections of neinei (*Dracophyllum latifolium*) amongst the generally dominant red beech trees. After the climb, the track begins an extensive sidle quite some distance from the lake, which is not reached again until you're at Sandy Bay. Eventually, a side track branches off to Kaipo Lagoon, signalling that you're just 10 minutes from the hut.

Sandy Bay is, indeed, pleasantly sandy, making a good surface underfoot for swimming, although it's rarely warm. In winter, this can be a cold place, and it's not that unusual for snow to fall right down to the lake edge. The hut sits just back from the shore, a three-roomed affair with two bunkrooms on either side of a kitchen area. Its veranda offers a great place from which to observe the lake during the evening – providing the sandflies are not too fierce.

A good side trip from Sandy Bay, which takes about an hour each way, is to Kaipo Lagoon, the remnant of a once larger lake that has slowly become silted up to form a wetland. This will eventually also be the fate of Lake Waikareiti, which is gradually becoming shallower as sediments are washed in by surrounding streams. The start of the track passes through some fine stands of red beech forest, surely the stateliest of New Zealand's four species of *Nothofagus*, and you pass some attractive wetlands containing *Dracophyllum*, *Gleichenia* ferns and sphagnum moss. Spider nursery-webs are common here, too.

For your return to Aniwaniwa from Sandy Bay, the Ruapani Track makes a good alternative, although it will take two hours longer. This delightful, benched track passes more small lakes and a couple of wetlands, which are small breaks in the otherwise extensive forest canopy. Lake Ruapani is the largest of these and is situated about halfway back to Aniwaniwa. Providing botanical interest on this walk are some stands of kahikatea around the lakes and more stands of neinei.

Forest on the Ruapani Track

Manuoha

Duration 2 days

Grade Medium

Times Road to Manuoha Hut (6 bunks, wood stove, $5/night): 5–6 hours

Maps W18 Waikaremoana, Te Urewera Parkmap

Access The Manuoha Track is located about half a kilometre north of the Hopuruahine Road turnoff, on SH 38; about 1 hour 45 minutes drive east from Murupara and 1 hour 20 minutes drive west from Wairoa. Trampers wanting to complete the track from Manuoha Hut to Lake Waikareiti are best advised to leave their vehicle at the Waikaremoana motorcamp and take a water taxi to the Hopuruahine landing.

Alternative Route For those with an extra day, the tramp to Manuoha can be linked with that around Lake Waikareiti (see previous walk). From Manuoha Hut to Sandy Bay Hut takes about 6–8 hours.

Information DOC Aniwaniwa Area Office, Ph 06 837 3803, urewerainfo@doc.govt.nz

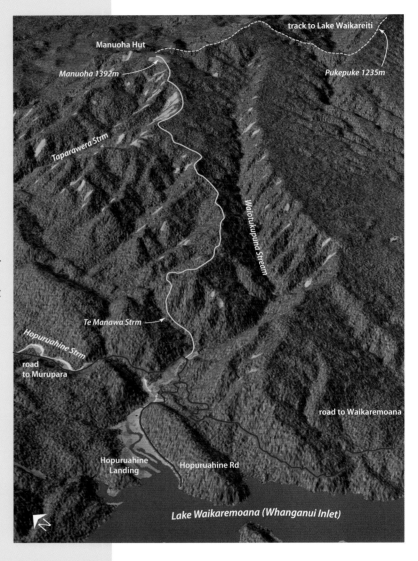

At 1392 metres, Manuoha is the highest point in Te Urewera National Park and pokes just above the bushline. The top offers extensive views, and the ridge track to it passes through some of the most exquisite forest in the park. While the track is not hard, it is reasonably long and not one for those who don't enjoy forest.

From its signposted start, the track enters the forest immediately and soon crosses

Te Manawa Stream. This provides the only water on the track, so it pays to fill your bottle here.

A steady climb ensues as the track ascends some steepish bush faces towards the ridge. At first, a mix of broadleaf trees including tawari combine with red and silver beech, but once you reach the ridge proper – after about an hour – silver beech begins to dominate. The well-marked track suffered extensive damage in a 2006 winter snowstorm, but has since been cleared.

The ridge is generally broad and undulating, the sort that would be a real navigational challenge without the track. Especially in light rain, travel through this forest is an almost primeval experience, the large silver beech trees heavily draped in lichens and moss, with the steady click and plop of water falling on leaves and branches. Rather than cutting a straight line, the track weaves around the larger trees. A few descents through several shallow dips are the only interruption to a slow gain in altitude, though overall you gain only 375 metres over approximately 7 kilometres of ridge.

Higher up, the beech trees grow perceptibly smaller. Numerous branches lie strewn on the forest floor, testimony not only to the ridge's exposure to gales, but also a sign of how heavily weighted they are when laden with moss. With a gain in altitude, the track gets progressively muddier, corresponding to the higher rainfall. After a brief narrow section of the ridge, where there are views over some extensive slips into the Taparawera Stream, the trees become increasingly gnarled. Broadleaf, leatherwood and pink pine begin to make an appearance, and the forest grows quite dark.

Just below the summit of Manuoha, the goblin forest reaches a zenith of twistedness, with long beards of moss growing thickly over

Mist in silver beech forest

everything. Under winter snow, it looks truly fantastical. Then, for a brief moment, you break out onto the tops, where a swimming pool-sized scrap of subalpine plants grows around the summit trig station. Amongst others, the vegetation includes leatherwood, *Dracophyllum*, hebe, coprosma and mountain celery pine. On a good day there are fine views south and east of Lake Waikaremoana, and beyond to Poverty and Hawke Bays. To the west lie Mt Ruapehu and Lake Taupo, while the forested and broken expanse of Te Urewera stretches to the north.

A short distance down the other side of the summit you plunge back into forest, where Manuoha Hut lies just five minutes from the trig. It's a small, tidy hut, although it can be damp. The following day, the return downhill trip proves significantly easier and is likely to take an hour or so less than the ascent. Those wanting a round trip could take an extra day and use the marked route that connects Manuoha with Lake Waikareiti over Pukepuke. Be aware though, that this is a long day and the track is considerably harder.

Tramper, Manuoha track

Hikurangi

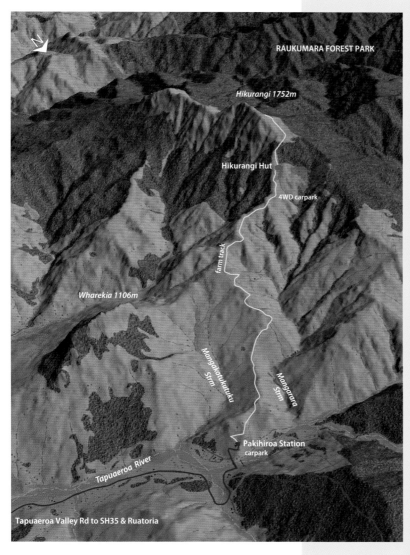

RAUKUMARA FOREST PARK

Hikurangi 1752m

Hikurangi Hut

4WD carpark

farm track

Wharekia 1106m

Mangaokutuku Strm

Mangarara Strm

Pakihiroa Station carpark

Tapuaeroa River

Tapuaeroa Valley Rd to SH35 & Ruatoria

Duration 2–3 days

Grade Medium–Hard

Times Roadend to Hikurangi Hut (12 bunks, wood stove, $15/night): 3.5–4 hours. Hut to summit of Hikurangi: 2 hours.

Map Y15 Hikurangi

Access From Gisborne, drive north along SH 35 to Ruatoria. Just north of the town, turn left onto Tapuaeroa Valley Road. Follow this for some 18 km to its end at Pakihiroa Station, where there's a carpark. Permission must be sought from Te Runanga o Ngati Porou to use the Hikurangi Hut. The tramp is now a gazetted walkway and access is possible all year round, except when it's closed by the iwi for lambing or for spiritual reasons. Closures are advertised in advance and can occur on a maximum of 50 days per year.

Alternative Route If the big climb over farmland doesn't appeal, Ngati Porou offer a guided trip onto the mountain, or can arrange a 4WD drop-off to within about 20 minutes walk of the hut.

Information DOC Gisborne, Ph 06 869 0460; Ngati Porou Visitor Centre, 144 Waiomatatini Road, Ruatoria, Ph 06 864 8660; www.ngatiporou.com

Te Ara ki Hikurangi, the sacred mountain of east coast iwi Ngati Porou, stands as a sentinel on East Cape, overlooking what is possibly the most rugged area of the North Island – the Raukumara Range. One translation of Hikurangi (which was named after a mountain in Hawaiki) is 'the end of the sky', and legends explain that the peak was the first place to emerge when the mythological hero Maui fished up the North Island. Hikurangi is also famous for being the first point on mainland New Zealand to see the sun.

Spaniard (speargrass) on the flanks of Hikurangi

Hikurangi's other distinguishing characteristic is less well known. At 1752 metres, it's the highest non-volcanic peak in the North Island and forms the summit of the great chain of mountains that stretches from East Cape to Wellington's Rimutaka Range.

The tramp begins at Pakihiroa Station near the head of the Tapuaeroa Valley, and a long slog ensues up farmed hillsides towards the distant bush boundary and hut. The route follows a clearly marked and defined farm track, but it's a demanding and thirsty 1000-metre climb, so take plenty of water. Any farm gates you pass through should be left as you find them, and use fence stiles where they are provided. On the ascent, there are increasingly good views of the northern Raukumara Forest Park and the severely eroded hills of this part of the east coast. Eventually, at about the 1100-metre contour, the road ends at a large carpark.

Here, in the late 1990s, Ngati Porou erected nine impressive whakairo, or carvings. While displaying traditional design elements, these carvings are undeniably modern and represent Maui and his whanau (family). Designed by artist Derek Lardelli, the whakairo add a fascinating cultural element to the tramp.

From the carpark follow marker poles through gaunt totara stumps, the remains of a forest that once stretched down the mountain's northern flanks. Hikurangi Hut, situated at an altitude of 1200 metres, offers commanding views and forms a convenient base from which to venture further onto Hikurangi. The Gisborne Canoe and Tramping Club built the hut in 1960–61, on Pakihiroa Station land that is now administered by Ngati Porou.

To climb Hikurangi, allow a good half-day, and set out only in reasonable weather. Beyond the hut, there are over 500 metres to climb to the top. Marker poles lead up a steep grassy slope into the forest above. Here, you climb more gently through silver beech forest into subalpine scrub and finally emerge above the bushline. There's a tarn here, surrounded by the dead limbs of leatherwood burnt in earlier fires. Good views unfold of the rugged Raukumara interior, with the precipitous summits of Whanokao to the northwest – its highest peak proved so rugged that it remained unclimbed until 1946, when Colin McLeron and Adrian Primrose reached the top. Altogether it's harsh country, and off-track travel here is only for those who particularly enjoy a good thrashing.

Above the bushline, a poled route leads across tussock slopes dotted with the occasional clump of speargrass. As well as these prickly plants, the community of alpine flora includes eyebrights, North Island edelweiss, everlasting daisies and the buttercup

Ranunculus insignis. In botanical terms, these plants are of extra interest because many of them reach their northern limit here.

The well-poled route leads across the mountain's western flanks. From these slopes Hikurangi has the appearance of a craggy massif rather than a single peak, and as yet the summit's exact location remains unclear. Eventually, you reach the base of a steep, rocky gully flanked by angular precipices. The route clambers up this gully, climbing a mixture of loose scree and more stable vegetated steps, until the summit ridge is gained.

Beyond, the track heads southeast on the narrow ridge, with steep drop-offs to the east. This final section can be daunting for those who don't like moderate exposure, and an overhanging speargrass offers a prickly resistance at the narrowest point. Under winter snows this ascent would be a serious undertaking, requiring some deft work with crampons and ice axe. Finally, the ridge broadens into a rocky summit, topped by a battered wooden trig station.

The views from the summit prove extensive, expanding on those already seen. One striking peak, a forested remnant lying marooned in farmland to the northeast, is the pyramid-like Wharekia. From the top you can also appreciate how far east Hikurangi lies from the main Raukumara Range, something of an anomaly for the highest peak in the area.

Whether you climb the peak in one day or overnight at the hut first, an ascent of Hikurangi is a big climb, and you cannot fail to be impressed by the ruggedness of the terrain and the aura that surrounds the place.

Maori whakairo, Hikurangi

Koranga River

Duration 2–3 days

Grade Medium

Times Moanui Road to Tawa Hut (6 bunks, open fire, $5/night): 3–4 hours. Tawa Hut to Koranga Forks Hut (6 bunks, open fire, $5/night) via Kahunui Stream: 4–5 hours. Koranga Forks Hut to Moanui Road: 2.5–3 hours.

Maps W17 Urewera, Te Urewera Parkmap

Access Some 67 km from Opotiki turn off SH 2 (the Waioeka Gorge section) onto Tewera Road. Follow this for 1 km, then take the Moanui Road. Continue for about 20 km to where DOC signs indicate the start of the track beside the Koranga River.

Alternative Route If high river levels make the round trip inadvisable, trampers can walk in and out to Koranga Forks Hut from Moanui Road.

Information DOC Opotiki Area Office, Ph 07 315 1001

This tramp through the backblocks of Gisborne's Waioeka Conservation Area is rarely used by anyone other than locals, but thoroughly deserves more attention. The 39,200-hectare conservation area straddles the Waioeka Gorge and lies between Te Urewera National Park to the southwest and the Raukumara Range to the north. The route incorporates two tidy huts, a beautiful river and a good chance to see blue ducks.

The tramp starts near the end of the convoluted, gravelly Moanui Road, in what must be one of Gisborne's most isolated farms, a small pocket of land hacked out of the surrounding bush. Journey's End Station marks the beginning of a 2–3 day trip along the Kahunui Stream and Koranga River, both tributaries of the Waioeka River.

From the DOC signpost, a track leads off through farmland and then bush on the true right of the Koranga River. After about a kilometre you reach a signposted track junction. Head left and descend briefly to where a swingbridge crosses the river. From here, you begin a climb up a poled route on a steepish farm track that the locals call, appropriately enough, 'The Burn' (it sure gets the calf muscles). This ends at a forested saddle, from where you begin a descent to the Kahuiti Stream.

The pleasant benched trail leads down through tawa forest, until the babble of the

Kahuiti Stream drowns the sound of the forest birds. About a kilometre downstream from where the Kahuiti merges with the Kahunui Stream, the track reaches Tawa Hut, a tidy six-bunk affair in a grassy clearing. There's ample camping nearby.

While this first day's stroll through the dark depths of the tawa forest comes as a cool change from other tramps in beech forest, it's the second day that will likely prove the most enjoyable. About a kilometre downstream of Tawa Hut the track ends, forcing you to take to the river. Here, deep pools swirl beside cascading rapids in a steep-sided gorge, and certainly on the map the river looks like it might require considerable swimming. It is indeed as twisted and steep-sided as the map indicates, writhing through a series of spectacularly green pools, but river crossing proves easy on gravelly sections just upstream of each set of rapids. While not to be underestimated after rain, when it quickly becomes impassable, during normal flow the river provides good travel.

In winter, the sun barely penetrates the gorge, and it can be cold going. However, like neighbouring Te Urewera National Park, the rivers here make an ideal habitat for blue ducks, and on at least one section you are quite likely to encounter some of these steel-grey birds.

The closed valley finally opens out at the junction with the Koranga River, where Koranga Forks Hut is situated. From this point, the river becomes the Waioeka and continues to gather strength until it emerges at the Waioeka Gorge on SH 2.

Kahunui Stream, Waioeka Conservation Area

The last day involves a scenic walk up an excellent benched track beside the Koranga River back to the Moanui Road end. Just upstream of the hut, the track initially crosses a swingbridge, then sidles along the true right of the river, passing through one small section of cleared land before plunging back into bush for the final 2 kilometres to the roadend. When the Koranga is in high flow, you might spot the occasional party of kayakers or rafters heading downstream for the Waioeka Gorge.

While access to this tramp can be rather long and tedious, the scenery and remoteness make it well worthwhile, and as a round trip it's even more appealing.

Whio, or blue duck, Hymenolaimus malacorhynchos

Syme Hut

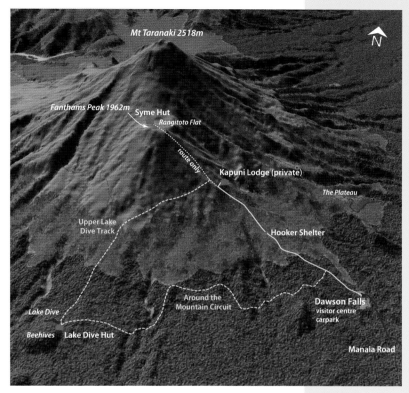

Duration 2 days

Grade Medium–Hard

Times Dawson Falls to Hooker Shelter: 40–60 minutes. Shelter to Syme Hut (12 bunks, $5/night): 2–3 hours.

Maps P20 Egmont, Egmont National Park Map

Access From SH 3 at Stratford turn left onto Opunake Road, and follow this for 15 km, then turn right onto Manaia Road. This leads into the park and beyond to the Dawson Falls Visitor Centre, where there's a carpark, information, toilets and a shelter.

Alternative Route For a longer tramp you could return to Dawson Falls via Lake Dive.

Information DOC Dawson Falls, Ph 025 430 248; DOC Stratford, Ph 06 765 5144

Syme Hut is arguably the most spectacularly sited hut in the North Island and offers trampers exceptional views of Mt Taranaki and the surrounding area. It's the highest hut in Egmont National Park and lies perched on the 1962-metre Fanthams Peak (Panitahi), a subsidiary volcanic cone lying just to the south of Mt Taranaki's main summit. While in summer this is a strenuous but straightforward tramp, during winter mountaineering skills are required.

The tramp begins at the Dawson Falls Visitor Centre, where you can get an updated weather forecast. Quite a number of short walks and track junctions exist in this area, but you can't go wrong if you follow signs saying 'summit'. The track plunges immediately into dense forest typical of Egmont National Park. Like many other North Island volcanic peaks – including Mt Tarawera, Pirongia, Karioi and Maungatautari – there's no beech forest on the mountain, and the dominant trees are instead kamahi, Hall's totara and broadleaf. In places, the moss-heavy branches of multi-stemmed kamahi interlock to give the vegetation its so-called 'goblin forest' appearance.

On the climb upward, those unfamiliar with the tracks of Egmont National Park will

Syme Hut and Mt Taranaki at dawn

soon come to know one of their classic characteristics: the hundreds of steps, often just wider than your stride. These were designed not so much with the human leg in mind, but as a means of reducing the erosion of the park's notoriously fragile soils.

By the time you reach Hooker Shelter, an open three-sided affair, the forest has been reduced to subalpine scrub, mainly dominated by leatherwood. Higher up, past the turn-off to Kapuni Lodge (a locked ski lodge belonging to the Mt Egmont Alpine Club), you reach tussock. The steps continue, climbing ever upwards. On a good day you'll soon have views over the vivid green patchwork of Taranaki farms and the startlingly sharp boundary of the park edge.

Eventually, the steps give out onto the scoria slopes of Fanthams Peak. Here, growing in compact patches, are hardy mosses, some of the highest growing plants on the mountain. Poles lead for some distance up these slopes, which reach their steepest just below the crest of the peak. In winter, this section can be very icy and quite treacherous to those without the appropriate skills and equipment. After gaining the crest, poles sidle above Rangitoto Flat – the expansive dip lying between Fanthams Peak and the southern slopes of Mt Taranaki itself.

Syme Hut is reached soon after. Views from here are simply sublime, particularly at dawn and dusk. Before you, looking deceptively steep, are the southern slopes of Mt Taranaki, while to the south and west is the great arc of the Taranaki Bight. Far to the east lie the forested hinterland of inland Taranaki and, on the far horizon, Mts Ruapehu and Ngauruhoe. At dawn, their far-flung summits are often suspended above an ocean of cloud, and in such conditions the sunrise from Syme Hut must surely be one of the best in the country. And at night you can watch the twinkling lights of several Taranaki towns, including Hawera, Stratford and Opunake.

Syme Hut itself has bunk space for 12, and while there's no heating it's quite cosy.

The current hut (constructed in 1987–88) replaced the original Syme Hut, first built in 1929–30 by the Mt Egmont Alpine Club. The death of two climbers high on the southern slopes of Taranaki in 1928 prompted local mountain enthusiasts to form the club, and one of their first projects was to construct a shelter on Fanthams Peak. It was named after Rod Syme, one of the club's founders and an active member of the team that built the hut. Unfortunately, due to poor placement the hut frequently became buried by snow and had to be rebuilt in 1953 and again in 1970. By 1986 it was badly deformed, leaking and considered beyond repair. Materials from the old hut were kept and now form part of the entrance to an audio-visual display room in the Dawson Falls Visitor Centre, a partial 're-creation' of the old Syme Hut.

Many people use Syme Hut as a base for climbing Mt Taranaki, and in the right conditions this is a relatively straightforward ascent. However, the climb is not to be underestimated and should be tackled only by those with sufficient experience. Those not wanting to attempt the summit can instead spend the morning exploring the large boulders of Rangitoto Flat and Fanthams Peak itself. The peak, sometimes called a parasitic cone, was formed after lava beneath the main volcano found its way through a weak point to create a secondary vent. It was named after Fanny Fantham, who became the first European woman to climb it back in March 1887, when she was just nineteen.

The tramp back down to Dawson Falls naturally takes considerably less time than the ascent, although there is the option of branching off on the Lake Dive Track. This leads across the lower flanks of Fanthams Peak to Lake Dive and the Lake Dive Hut, and then back to the visitor centre on part of the lower Around-the-Mountain Circuit.

Dawn over Ngauruhoe and Ruapehu from Fanthams Peak

Pouakai Range

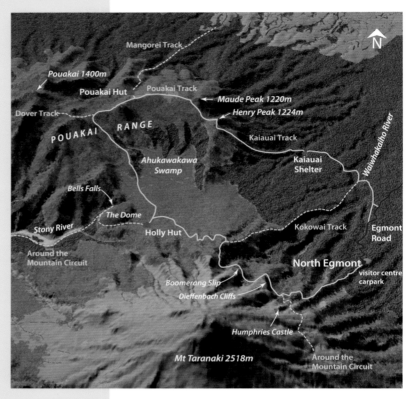

EGMONT NATIONAL PARK

Duration 2 days

Grade Medium

Times North Egmont to Holly Hut (32 bunks, woodstove, $15/night): 3–4 hours. Side trip to Bells Falls: 30 minutes each way. Holly Hut to Pouakai Hut (16 bunks, woodstove, $15/night): 2–3 hours. Pouakai Hut to North Egmont 4–5 hours.

Maps P20 Egmont, Egmont Parkmap

Access From just west of Egmont Village, on SH 3, turn onto Egmont Road, and follow it to the carpark at the North Egmont Visitor Centre. Here you will find information, toilets and the historic Camphouse, a 32-bunk hut that can be booked for accommodation.

Alternative Route You can also reach Pouakai Hut via the Mangorei Track, which starts from Mangorei Road, south of New Plymouth. This is a shorter track (2–3 hours each way to the hut) and a better poor-weather alternative, but has the disadvantage of not being a round trip.

Information DOC Taranaki Area Office, Ph 06 759 0350; Egmont National Park Visitor Centre, Ph 06 756 0990

Mt Taranaki is the sort of mountain you never tire of looking at, and one of the best places to view it from is the neighbouring Pouakai Range. Lying to the north of Mt Taranaki, the range is distant enough to give vantage points not found on the flanks of the mountain itself. From here, you can enjoy looking across at Mt Taranaki, instead of the neck-straining view most often experienced on the Around-the-Mountain Circuit.

This excellent weekend tramp accesses the Pouakai Range using the northern part of the Around-the-Mountain Circuit, and ends back at North Egmont. It's a great round trip, traversing all the varied terrain in this northern part of Egmont National Park.

From the North Egmont carpark near The Camphouse, take the Veronika Loop Track, which plunges into forest immediately, beginning a steep climb onto a razorback ridge. At a track junction (where the Veronika Loop Track branches off) keep heading uphill. After crossing a couple of gullies, you intercept the high level Around-the-Mountain Circuit, where you should head right. Humphries Castle, a popular crag for rock climbers, forms a distinctive landmark, with the profile of Mt Taranaki beyond. Here the close views of Taranaki lack the grandeur and symmetry of the views that await you on the Pouakai Range.

Mt Taranaki from Pouakai Range

The track passes beneath the angular columns of the Dieffenbach Cliffs, then continues sidling around to cross Boomerang Slip – named for its shape. Despite the somewhat barren, volcanic landscapes, there's sufficient shelter for foxgloves to thrive. Elsewhere lichens and mosses have colonised boulders.

About halfway to Holly Hut, past a signposted turnoff to the Kokowai Track, the benched track sidles across a series of gorges cut by numerous streams radiating like spokes from Mt Taranaki. Finally, there's a long but gradual descent to Holly Hut. The hut is located about 10 minutes past the junction where the track to the Pouakai Range branches off the main Around-the-Mountain Circuit. The comfortable Holly Hut is the largest in Egmont National Park. If energy levels permit, shed your packs and make the worthwhile 30-minute detour to Bells Falls, where the Stony River thunders over a lava plug known as The Dome.

From Holly Hut, head back to the track junction and begin a gentle descent towards the Ahukawakawa Swamp, formed when debris flows blocked the Stony River. The landscape seems more liquid than solid – spongy, sodden and crowded with red tussock, mountain flax, sphagnum moss and a mosaic of other wetland plants adapted to survive the acidic conditions. A long series of boardwalks lead across the swamp to the Stony River.

After crossing the Stony River on an arched footbridge, a series of steps lead up through forest dominated by stunted pahautea (mountain cedar) onto the exposed tops of the Pouakai Range. Increasingly good views of Mt Taranaki expand as you gain height.

There can be few places where a single mountain so dominates a landscape as the aloof and isolated Taranaki. Once, some 250,000 years ago, there was a Pouakai volcano that had a similar profile and height to Mt Taranaki. Today's Pouakai Range is the remnant lower slopes of that volcanic cone, whittled to its present shape by the erosive action of rivers and ice.

Once on the range crest, the route to the Dover Track branches off to the west. Head right for about 20 minutes along the range, until a five-minute track branches off to Pouakai Hut. This sizeable hut makes a good destination for the night, with the balcony sporting a vista of New Plymouth and the northern Taranaki Bight.

If the weather permits, it's worthwhile rising early and heading back to the crest of the Pouakai Range to witness the sunrise on the mountain. Sometimes, the Ahukawakawa Swamp is obscured under an ocean-like layer of low cloud.

Beyond the knoll above the hut, the track leads across a flattish section of tops, past some small tarns, which often reflect Mt Taranaki in some splendour. Eyebrights and foxgloves are abundant, and beyond loom the hooded shapes of Henry and Maude. A sidle leads around the southern slopes of Maude, but a series of wooden steps surmount the gnarled knuckle of Henry. On top there's a large wooden platform with another fine view of Mt Taranaki and the Ahukawakawa Swamp.

More wooden steps descend from Henry, through a band of Egmont leatherwood (*Brachyglottis rotundifolia*) towards the forest encasing the lower slopes. This transition from the subalpine tops into the forest is always a sharp change; from expansiveness and views to a shaded, enclosed environment – or sometimes from full-on exposure to the elements to a dripping, filtered rain.

Stands of conical pahautea dominate the forest at first, but lower down are kamahi and Hall's totara, and then finally Northern rata and podocarps. The three-sided Kaiauai Shelter provides a place for respite from the elements if the weather proves inclement, or just a handy excuse for a snack. After crossing a stream (which can be impassable when flooded) near the shelter, the track sidles across more forested slopes – intersected by some deep gullies – before descending to the Waiwhakaiho River, which is spanned by a swingbridge near the confluence with Ram Stream. From here the Ram Track ascends a spur towards the road. Either end at the Kaiauai carpark (about a 2-kilometre walk along the road up to the carpark); or continue up the Ram Track to North Egmont.

Tramper crosses Ahukawakawa Swamp

Ascent of Mt Taranaki

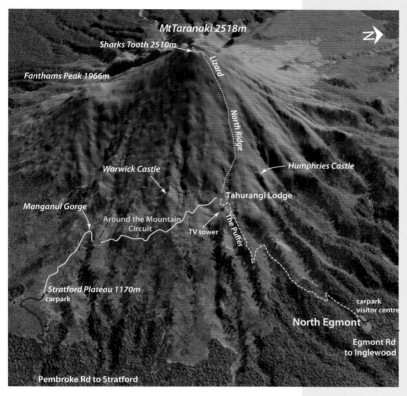

Mt Taranaki 2518m
Sharks Tooth 2510m
Fanthams Peak 1966m
Lizard
North Ridge
Warwick Castle
Humphries Castle
Tahurangi Lodge
Manganui Gorge
Around the Mountain Circuit
TV tower
The Puffer
Stratford Plateau 1170m carpark
carpark visitor centre
North Egmont
Egmont Rd to Inglewood
Pembroke Rd to Stratford

Duration 1 day

Grade Hard–Mountaineering

Times From Stratford Plateau to Tahurangi Lodge (locked): 1.5–2 hours. Tahurangi Lodge to summit: 3–4 hours. Return from summit to Stratford Plateau: 3–4 hours.

Maps P20 Egmont, Egmont Parkmap

Access Turn off SH 3 at Stratford onto Pembroke Road, and follow this for about 18 km to Stratford Plateau, where there's a carpark.

Alternative Route You can also start from North Egmont, but while this is shorter in distance, it involves more climbing.

Information DOC Taranaki Area Office, Ph 06 759 0350; Egmont National Park Visitor Centre, Ph 06 756 0990

In New Zealand, Mt Taranaki is undoubtedly the mountain most isolated from others. Lying alone on the semi-circle of the Taranaki Bight, it commands a presence few other peaks can match, forming an irresistible attraction for climbers. An ascent of the 2518-metre-high volcano is something many trampers aspire to, but it is most emphatically not a peak to underestimate. Over 60 people have died on its slopes – many of them ill-prepared trampers – and together with Aoraki/Mt Cook, Mt Taranaki vies for the position of New Zealand's most lethal mountain. That said, Mt Taranaki offers unsurpassed views, and on one of those days when fluffy coastal cloud drapes the lower slopes, an ascent leaves you seemingly suspended 'between heaven and earth'.

In the right conditions, during summer or early autumn, it's a fairly straightforward tramp up steepish scree slopes on the mountain's north side into the summit crater, then a scramble up onto the rocky summit itself. However, in winter or spring this is certainly not a tramp, but rather a mountaineering trip. Another factor to consider is Mt Taranaki's close proximity to the sea. As the major topographical barrier in the region, the mountain literally attracts storms, and even those familiar with New Zealand's notoriously unpredictable climate can underestimate the speed with which weather changes here. Parties tackling Mt Taranaki need to be well prepared for any weather conditions, and even during summer trampers should carry an ice axe and start early.

Stream and foxgloves, Ourisia spp, Egmont National Park

Although the most direct route starts from North Egmont, the trip described here begins from Stratford Plateau as this offers a higher altitude (1170 m) from which to start your ascent. From the carpark on the plateau, join the upper level of the Around-the-Mountain Circuit, and head anticlockwise. Initially, the track ascends beside the deep gouge of the Manganui Gorge, site of some of the mountain's largest avalanches (it pays to seek advice about avalanche conditions before beginning your trip). Once across the gulch, the track sidles northwards, passing by the locked Manganui Ski Lodge and through some delightful alpine herbfields. During early summer, the area is alive with the blooms of the delicate Mt Egmont foxglove, which is endemic to Taranaki, and the yellow snow buttercup.

Further around, you pass the imposing prow of Warwick Castle, one of the mountain's top rock-climbing crags. Further on still, at the top of 'The Puffer' (a steep access road used to service a television transmission tower), you reach Tahurangi Lodge. This Taranaki Alpine Club hut is often locked, but if there are club members present you may be able to fill up your water bottles here. Either way, carry plenty of water, as there is still a long ascent ahead. At Tahurangi Lodge you leave the Around-the-Mountain Circuit and begin a climb up a series of wooden stairs towards the North Ridge.

These eventually give out onto steepish scoria slopes, which lead almost all the way to the summit. On a good summer's day there is usually a fair number of people heading for the top, and the route is often quite well defined. However, in poor visibility, climbers have lost their way and come to grief. There are a few poles lower down, but none higher up.

For those who are less experienced, the loose footholds in the scree take some getting used to, but upward progress comes steadily enough. This North Ridge route was the one used by the German explorer Ernst Dieffenbach in 1839. His successful climb up Mt Taranaki with James Heberley was the first alpine ascent in New Zealand's recorded European history, although Maori had undoubtedly reached the summit during earlier centuries.

Views expand as you gain height, with New Plymouth prominent to the north and, closer, the tops of the Pouakai Range and Ahukawakawa Swamp. Ahead, the snag of the Sharks Tooth is prominent on the left, looking at this point higher than the actual summit. Aim for a prominent gap on its right. The steepest part comes just before you crest the lip of the crater, where the more solid rock of the Lizard provides surer footing. After pausing for breath and a snack on the crater rim, it's just a few minutes' scramble up rocks onto the summit. Here you're at the apex of Egmont National Park, which is scribed in a circle of surrounding forest, perfectly round save for the protrusion of the Kaitake Range. The views are astounding, and on a clear day vast tracts of the North Island are visible, and even the northern part of the South Island.

Mt Taranaki may seem extinct, but it's really just dormant. The last eruption, in 1755, occurred less than a century before Dieffenbach's climb, and an earlier 1655 eruption destroyed the nearby fortified pa of Karaka. However, on a breathlessly calm, fine day, the summit seems to be a place of profound peace, one where you are far above the world and feel gloriously insignificant.

In summer, the descent is often an exhilarating scree run, but even the scree can become treacherous when frozen. The descent is usually the most dangerous part of any climb, and gravity awaits those moments when tiredness might relax your vigilance. If any snow lies on the summit, you'll need that ice axe, possibly crampons and, of course, the experience to use them safely.

Once back at Tahurangi Lodge, the contours become kinder on knees once again. After some 1350 metres of ascent and descent, the walk back to Stratford Plateau is likely to be accomplished with slightly less spring in your step, but you'll savour the satisfaction of having climbed the second-highest mountain in the North Island.

Climber descending from the summit of Mt Taranaki, with the Sharks Tooth beyond

Matemateaonga Track

Duration 3–4 days

Grade Easy–Medium

Times Kohi Saddle to Omaru Hut (8 bunks, woodstove, $15/night): 1.5–2 hours. Omaru to Mt Humphries turn-off: 3 hours. Ascent of Mt Humphries: 1.5 hours return. Turn-off to Pouri Hut (12 bunks, woodstove, $15/night): 1.5 hours. Pouri Hut to Ngapurua Shelter: 4–4.5 hours. Ngapurua to Puketotara Hut (8 bunks, woodstove, $15/night): 3.5 hours. Puketotara to Whanganui River: 1 hour.

Maps R20 Matemateaonga, Whanganui Parkmap

Access Turn off SH 3 at Stratford onto SH 43. Follow this for 30 km until you reach Strathmore. Turn right and follow the road for 8 km to the junction of Upper and Lower Mangaehu roads. Turn left here (towards Aotuhia), from where it's 16 km to Kohi Saddle and the start of the track. Prior to departure, you'll need to arrange a jetboat pick-up at the eastern end of the track on the Whanganui River. Some companies can arrange your transport for both ends.

Information DOC Wanganui Area Office, Ph 06 349 2100

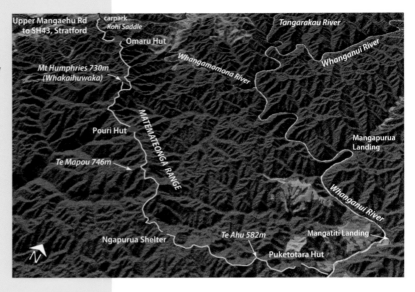

The 42-kilometre Matemateaonga Track is an old Maori route that traverses the heart of the North Island's second-largest expanse of native forest, that of Whanganui National Park and the neighbouring Waitotara Conservation Area. The track begins a considerable distance inland from the Taranaki town of Stratford and ends somewhere even more remote, right on the banks of the Whanganui River. Although the walk can be accomplished in as little as two days, most parties require at least another day or two, given the difficult and time-consuming transport arrangements.

From Kohi Saddle, a large sign and stile indicate the start of the track, which is often very muddy until a second stile is crossed onto the track proper. It's a pleasure to walk on this well-benched track which follows a remarkably even gradient along the Matemateaonga Range. Nowhere (excepting the short side trip to Mt Humphries) does the track climb more than about 20 metres, a fact made less surprising once you realise it follows the original route of a never-completed road. The track now runs along what was intended to be the Whakaihuwhaka Road, linking Stratford with the main trunk line at Raetihi. Although a pilot track was cut in 1911, the outbreak of World War I ensured it was never widened, and the road suffered the same fate of many later settlement ventures in the Whanganui area – abandonment.

Aside from the easy gradient, another feature of the Matemateaonga that differentiates it from most other tramps is the presence of small marker posts every kilometre, each indicating the distance to Puketotara Hut. These serve a more useful gauge of your progress than you might imagine, because the easy gradient of the track means distances translate very well into time.

Omaru Hut lies well-situated only a couple of hours from the roadend and is as far as most parties want to go after the long drive in. Like the rest of those on the track, the hut was built in the early 1980s during a rash of enthusiasm that saw several tracks – including the Matemateaonga – upgraded and promoted as 'walkways', although officially the Matemateaonga has never been gazetted as one.

If you don't like bush, then the Matemateaonga probably isn't ideal, but for those who appreciate the dense, dark and almost claustrophobic nature of huge forest expanses it's a wonderful walk. Not that the forest is by any means uniform; in fact it's the subtle variations that create interest as you travel. Patches of wheki interrupt the canopy, which is dominated by northern rata and kamahi, with rewarewa, rimu, mahoe and hinau common in places. There are also some attractive stands of tawa, whose leaves form deep litter on the track. On some parts of the forest floor are impressive patches of *Dawsonia superba*, the world's tallest moss.

Roughly halfway between Omaru and Pouri huts lies the side track to Mt Humphries, at 730 metres the second-highest point in Whanganui National Park. The 1.5-hour return trip to the summit is worthwhile for the extensive vista: on a clear day Mt Taranaki and the peaks of Tongariro National Park are all plainly visible, as is the Whanganui River – a topographical

Northern rata tree, Matemateaonga Track

tribute to the Maori legend celebrating the links between all these features.

The day between Pouri and Puketotara huts is by far the longest on the tramp, but the conveniently positioned Ngapurua Shelter provides a good place for a lunch break, and there is water here too. DOC plans to replace the current shelter with a new 10-bunk serviced hut in 2009. By this stage you are right in the heart of the great forest, and it's really only the ease of the track that disguises your remoteness.

The fairly low, uniform height of the Matemateaonga Range and lack of tops disguises how rugged and remote the surrounding bush country really is. It's actually ancient peneplain, some one million years old, subsequently thrust up to its present height and now cut by numerous rivers, including the Whanganui, Omaru and Waitotara. Off-track travel is extremely arduous, with papa bluffs and deeply incised gorges to negotiate, not to mention the dense bush.

There are glimpses of this ruggedness from clearings along the track, often from the edge of slips or from numerous bridges that span small creeks. Despite the presence of these creeks, in summer you'd be well advised to carry some water as the track's position near the crest of the range can make it scarce.

Puketotara Hut lies only a couple of kilometres from the track end on the Whanganui River. This is the only section of track that descends notably, down a series of steps, through a couple of grassy clearings, then finally down more steps to a point where you first glimpse the river. The Whanganui itself has a character unique among New Zealand rivers, with papa cliffs, numerous waterfalls and a tangible presence of history. During floods, the water is often a chocolate milkshake colour, swirling with subdued power, and the level can rise or drop very quickly. Locals consider a 6-metre rise to be just a 'fresh'; 'floods' are considerably bigger!

The jetboat ride from the landing out to Pipiriki is undoubtedly one of the highlights of the trip, providing a snapshot experience of New Zealand's longest navigable river. Although the paddle-steamers may have gone, you are likely to pass some canoeists enjoying downstream travel.

Matemateaonga Track

Train's Hut

Duration 2 days

Grade Easy

Time Taumatatahi to Train's Hut (6 bunks, woodstove, $5/night): 4–6 hours

Maps R21 Ngamatapouri, R20 Matemateaonga

Access From SH 3 at Waitotara, turn onto Waitotara Valley Road. Follow it to Makakaho Junction, then turn left onto Taumatatahi Road. Follow this to the roadend, and park on a grassy area just before a bridge over the Waitotara River. Altogether, it's a long drive of some 57 km, the last 10 km of which is winding and metalled.

Alternative Route It's also possible to jetboat up the Waitotara River from Taumatatahi, to a point just below the Terereohaupa Falls. The ride can be arranged both ways, or as a 'jetboat in, walk out' trip, through the Taumatatahi-based operator Remote Adventures (www.remoteadventures.co.nz).

Information DOC Wanganui Area Office, Ph 06 349 2100

The tramp to Train's Hut in the Waitotara Conservation Area is one of those trips known only to a few Wanganui locals, but it deserves wider attention. From a remote farm in the upper Waitotara Valley, a well-benched track leads beside the Waitotara River to the old homestead at Kapara then on to Train's Hut. The area is interesting for its history, attractive forests and the underlying papa topography. As the hut lies at an altitude of only 100 metres it's never very cold even in winter, and the completely bridged track allows all-weather access. Altogether Train's Hut provides a good all-season destination.

From the grassy flat where you park your car, walk back to the last curve on the road and take the farm road leading through an open gate. Nearby, there's an inconspicuous sign that reads 'Train's Hut 5 hours'. A benched track which used to exist here was unfortunately bulldozed into a muddy road recently by the South Taranaki District Council, which manages the route as far as Kapara. At one point you pass an old rail slip – the first sign of past logging activity.

The Waitotara River itself is in some ways a smaller version of its much larger neighbour, the Whanganui, in that it is slow-moving, often brown and rarely without a partially submerged log or two on the bends. Covering the steep banks rising from the river are exceptionally green forests that include a verdant mix of northern rata, rimu, tawa, mahoe and nikau palms. There are North Island robins galore, often calling in their surprisingly loud and seemingly indignant manner.

After an hour or so you come across the dismantled remains of an old wooden bridge. In what I view as an act of vandalism, the South Taranaki District Council destroyed this wonderful old historic bridge, which used to be one of the highlights of the tramp. It was a symbol of past endeavour, which now you can only appreciate from the accompanying photograph.

Terereohaupa Falls, Waitotara River

Thankfully, due to the efforts of the late Arthur Bates (a Wanganui historian and tramper), the following history has been recorded. In the early days of the area's farming settlement, prior to the 1890s, transport was by horse or canoe. Later, a road was pushed through to its present end at Taumatatahi. One of the settlers, a South African Boer named William Van Asch, had taken up a remote holding at Kapara, and through the force of his personality managed to convince the authorities to extend the road to his homestead which lay a further 6 kilometres through wilderness. It's this old road that the track now follows, and the wooden bridge presumably dated from that era too.

You soon reach Kapara, at the junction of the Waitotara and one of its tributaries, where the remains of the homestead lie. Although Van Asch felled a considerable area of bush for his farm and built his own sawmill, he was obviously a man with some conservation ideals. He sold Kapara in 1912 but continued to be active in the region's politics. Thanks to his campaigning, a huge block of bush lying to the north of the Waitotara was designated a 'climatic reserve', reversing an earlier decision to divide it into sections. Thus was formed the basis for what is now the Waitotara Conservation Area.

The Kapara homestead is now largely in ruins, with a sagging and leaky roof, and it retains little of its former grandeur as a large house with an extensive garden and even a tennis court. It now looks forlorn and speaks volumes about hardship, ruin and lost dreams. Although the land is still private property, trampers can legally cross it on the designated track.

From Kapara, the track leads north towards the river and drops to cross a stream via a footbridge. This is the first of a number of gulches incised in the highly erodable papa that underlies the whole area. At this stage the track noticeably improves as you enter the Waitotara Conservation Area, which is under the management of DOC. Travel is pleasant along the well-benched track which passes through regenerating forest dominated by manuka and wheki. Several footbridges cross small streams, while two swingbridges cross larger ones. A reasonable grassy campsite appears about 15 minutes past the second swingbridge. On this section you're likely to encounter several wild goats, the scourge of the area and a major conservation problem.

About 15 minutes before Train's Hut, you pass the Terereohaupa Falls, an attractive cascade falling in a silky veil over an undercut papa bluff. Accessible on this side of the river is a good swimming hole beneath the falls. However those wanting an even better viewpoint to admire the cascade will need to access the opposite bank. This requires crossing a new suspension bridge located five minutes upstream, followed by a scramble downstream on an old, overgrown track for 20 minutes.

Like Kapara, the area around Train's Hut was once farmed, and the hut sits in a grassy clearing dotted with wheki. The hut is named after Fred Train, a Waitotara storekeeper, who was given the surrounding land in payment for a debt owed by the original settler. Train's sons tried to farm the area but left in 1922. According to Arthur Bates, the original Train's Hut even made headlines in the national newspapers once. The news concerned a

Old bridge, Waitotara Valley. This historic wooden bridge was photographed in 2001, about a year before it was dismantled.

plane crash, echoing the one that occurred at Armstrong Saddle in the Ruahines (see the Sunrise Hut route), although fortunately this one ended happily.

In December 1949, father and son Oswald and Ian Palmer crashed their Tiger Moth during a flight from Wanganui to New Plymouth. After the subsequent search they were given up for dead, but to the surprise of everyone the pair emerged out of the bush at Kapara 16 days after the accident. They'd survived the first six days' walk on three packets of chewing gum and were relieved to find food left by hunters at the old Train's Hut. After a rest at the hut, they summoned sufficient energy to continue to Kapara.

The current Train's Hut was built in 1990, and while not a great location, its porch does make a convenient place from which to listen for North Island brown kiwi at night. The following day you can retrace your footsteps, unless you've made arrangements for a jetboat pick-up from below the falls.

Waitotara River, Waitotara Conservation Area

TONGARIRO NATIONAL PARK

Tongariro Alpine Crossing

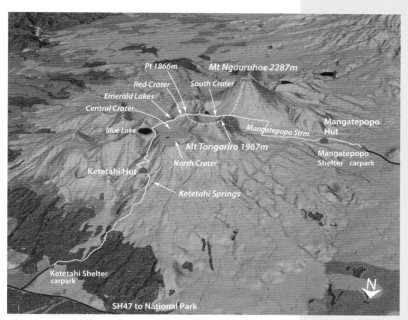

Duration 1–2 days

Grade Medium

Times Roadend to Ketetahi Hut (26 bunks, gas heater and cooking rings, $25/night): 2–3 hours. Ketetahi to Emerald Lakes: 1–2 hours. Emerald Lakes to Mangatepopo Hut (23 bunks, gas heater and cooking rings, $25/night): 3–4 hours. Side trip to Mt Ngauruhoe: 3 hours return. Mangatepopo Hut to roadend: 20 minutes. Note that Ketetahi and Mangatepopo are very popular Great Walk huts requiring a dated hut pass during the peak season between 1 October and 30 April. During the off-peak season the huts do not have gas heating or cooking facilities and cost $15/night. Campsites exist near both huts and cost $20/night (off-peak $5/night).

Maps T19 Tongariro, Tongariro Parkmap

Access From Turangi, drive south on SH 1 for 10 km, then turn onto SH 47. The small gravel side road to the Ketetahi carpark branches off on the left after about 15 km. The tramp ends at the Mangatepopo Shelter, at the end of the 6-km-long Mangatepopo Road accessible off SH 47. Many transport operators will arrange a drop-off and pick-up.

Alternative Route The Tongariro Northern Circuit Great Walk combines the Tongariro Crossing with the Tama Lakes tramp. Very fit trampers could accomplish this in a weekend, but most would want a more leisurely 3–4 days.

Information DOC Ruapehu Area Office, Ph 07 892 3729

The Tongariro Alpine Crossing has in recent decades become one of the most popular tramps in the country, and it's not hard to see why. This magnificent track crosses some of the most colourful and dramatic volcanic topography anywhere on the planet, with superb views and good huts. In many ways, the crossing encapsulates the World Heritage features of Tongariro National Park in a one or two day journey. If you've a hankering for volcanic landscapes, this is definitely the tramp to do.

Be warned, however, that during summer or on fine days you will meet a steady stream of people, and it's far from a 'wilderness' experience. It's also a very exposed tramp, and one that the less experienced often underestimate. You'll need to take warm and weatherproof clothing as the weather can change from arid to arctic very quickly. And in winter, skills with an ice axe and crampons may be necessary too.

Most people walking the track in a single day start from the Mangatepopo end, but if you plan to spend a night on the track, a stay at Ketetahi Hut probably makes more sense as this will break up the length of the days better. Either way, there are transport operators based at Whakapapa, Turangi and Taupo who can drop you off and pick you up at the other end.

Blue Lake and Mt Ngauruhoe at dawn

From the Ketetahi carpark, a well-gravelled track leads into forest and begins a gradual ascent. After crossing a stream over a footbridge, the track zigzags up a steeper section before suddenly emerging at the bushline. Ahead, steam rises from the Ketetahi Springs, dominated behind by the sharp edge of North Crater.

A gentle climb ensues through tussock landscapes, in places interrupted by introduced heather – purple when in flower – that is creeping around the park. As the slope steepens, you pass a sign marking an area of private land through which the track passes. The Ketetahi Hot Springs lie within this small parcel of land, which is owned by a local iwi, and trampers should respect their request not to visit the springs. The trail leads across some incised scoria gullies and ends with a short sidle to Ketetahi Hut. Perched with commanding views over Lake Rotoaira, Pihanga, Lake Taupo and the Kaimanawa mountains, it's no wonder that Ketetahi Hut is the one of the most popular huts in the country. During peak seasons, the hut and surrounding campsites can be very busy.

Above the hut, the trail begins an ascent into increasingly barren landscapes. Zigzags lead to a long sidle into Central Crater, a large depression as desolate as a moonscape. Nearby Blue Lake offers a dazzling circle of colour in a scene otherwise dominated by earthen tones. During summer there may be a sprinkling of *Ranunculus* buttercups here, sprouting butter-yellow flowers that are in stark contrast to their surroundings.

Poles lead across the expanse of Central Crater to a scene of exquisite beauty: the aptly named Emerald Lakes, set like jewels beneath the burnt pit of Red Crater. These are three old explosion pits now filled with highly acidic water of an arresting blue-green colour that changes hue according to the light and time of day. The colour of the lakes is caused by ions formed through the combination of water and minerals, mainly fumarolic sulphur.

A 'one-step-up, two-steps-down' scree climb leads up a ridge beside Red Crater to one of the outstanding viewpoints of the track. Pt 1886 is the high point of the track, both literally and figuratively. Here you can see the solid, symmetrical form of Mt Ngauruhoe rising starkly from South Crater, with Mt Ruapehu brooding and partially obscured behind. A side trail (allow an extra two hours return) leads to the summit of Mt Tongariro, at 1967 metres the lowest of the three major peaks in the park. To the north lies Pihanga, and far to the west you may be able to spot Mt Taranaki. Red Crater, an old magma dyke, steams quietly but menacingly close, its sulphur fumes lending the tramp a distinctly olfactory flavour. Altogether, it's both a visual validation for the famous Maori legend that links these peaks and an immensely creative and dynamic landscape to witness.

Once you've absorbed the power of the landscape here, a steady descent leads along a leading ridge to South Crater. After crossing this flat section of the tramp, you reach a lip overlooking the Mangatepopo Valley, a place dominated by sometimes weird shapes left from previous lava flows.

From the lip, there's the option of climbing Mt Ngauruhoe, an energy-sapping but rewarding side trip up steepish scree slopes (allow an extra three hours return). Otherwise, the remainder of the tramp is downhill, with a long sidle on a new section of track that crosses Mt Ngauruhoe's lower slopes. Down in the valley the track ambles above the Mangatepopo Stream, passing some toilets en route.

Some of the lava sculptures here resemble strange sea creatures, while other more stubby ones seem to have the less ominous appearance of garden gnomes. Several of these lava flows, originating from Mt Ngauruhoe, have occurred over the past couple of centuries, including two in 1870, one in 1949 and at least 10 during the 1954 eruptions.

Mangatepopo Hut appears on a small flat beside the stream, accessible via a two-minute side track. Beyond, it's just 20 minutes to the Mangatepopo Road, which marks the end of one of the North Island's truly classic tramps.

Emerald Lakes during winter, Tongariro National Park

Turoa–Whakapapa

TONGARIRO NATIONAL PARK

Duration 2–3 days

Grade Medium

Times Roadend to Manga-turuturu Hut (10 bunks, woodstove, $15/night): 1.5–2 hours. Mangaturuturu to Whakapapaiti Hut (16 bunks, woodstove, $15/night): 5.5–6 hours. Whakapapaiti to Whakapapa: 2.5 hours.

Maps S20 Ohakune, Tongariro Parkmap

Access From Ohakune, take the Ohakune Mountain Road which leads to Turoa Skifield. You pass the DOC Ohakune Visitor Centre a short distance out of town. The track begins above the A-frame Massey University Alpine Club Hut, at the road's 15 km mark – a point known as Wanganui Corner.

Alternative Route The tramp described is only part of the Ruapehu Round-the-Mountain Track, which normally takes 4–6 days.

Information DOC Ruapehu Area Office, Ph 07 892 3729

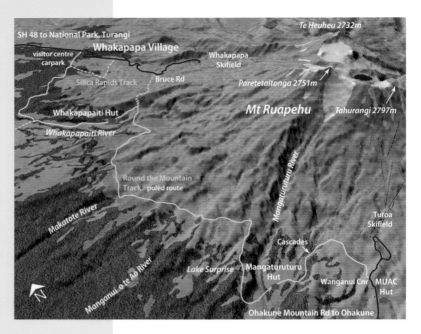

This tramp follows part of the Round-the-Mountain Track on the western slopes of Mt Ruapehu, between Turoa and Whakapapa. There's a mixture of tops and forest travel in this lesser-used part of the Tongariro National Park, with some fine views of Mt Ruapehu. En route are several waterfalls, one lake and two huts.

Although it is, of course, possible to walk the track in either direction, starting at the Ohakune Mountain Road means an overall descent, rather than an ascent. This also gives the advantage of a short first day, welcomed especially by those who've travelled some distance. From the road a signposted track follows poles across scoria slopes, with the bulky Mt Ruapehu dominating the eastern horizon. Here, three peaks of the volcano (Paretetaitonga, Tahurangi and Girdlestone) are apparent, giving it an altogether different profile to those views from the south or north.

The well-defined, poled track crosses two gullies and old lava flows, and climbs a low ridge above the Mangaturuturu Cascades. These are a series of cataracts rather than a single waterfall, tumbling down an unusual cream-coloured bed. The cream colour originates from silica deposited by the water, and with Mt Ruapehu behind, the falls make a photogenic foreground. Poles lead across the stream above the falls, from where you descend sharply along the adjacent ridge. Watch your footing here when the rocks are icy or wet. Below the cascades, flat walking leads to boardwalks across subalpine wetlands that end at Mangaturuturu Hut.

The hut lies on the edge of a patch of mountain beech forest, just across the river from some striking lava bluffs. Such settings that combine forest, alpine plants and views are always pleasant places to spend time. Mangaturuturu Hut was built in 1958 by the Wanganui Tramping Club, which, with DOC, still maintains it. It's a somewhat unusual though cosy design, with many-paned front windows positioned to show Mt Ruapehu to advantage.

The following day involves an exposed section of tramping that in winter or during stormy conditions could prove testing. Mt Ruapehu's volatility should not be forgotten either – this tramp is vulnerable to lahars, large flows of volcanic ash and

Alpine plants, Mangaturuturu Hut, Tongariro National Park

mud that can sweep down the mountainside at speeds of up to 50 kilometres per hour. During the 1995 eruptions, one of the 30-odd lahars that occurred destroyed a footbridge over the Whangaehu, on the southern part of the Round-the-Mountain Track. Lahars also channelled into both the Whakapapaiti and Mangaturuturu valleys.

From Mangaturuturu Hut, you first cross a branch of the Mangaturuturu River, which flows along the bed of an old lahar that swept down the valley in 1975. The river can be difficult to cross in high flow. Once across, the track begins a climb through mountain beech to Lake Surprise. Travelling in this direction, the shallow tarn of Lake Surprise won't be too startling, as you'll already have seen it from a distance the day before. On a fine, calm day it's a place to loiter, enjoying the reflections of Mt Ruapehu on the lake surface.

Above Lake Surprise, the track climbs a series of wooden steps before eventually emerging onto the more exposed scoria flanks of Mt Ruapehu. The tramp sidles across these flanks for the remainder of the day, crossing in and out of numerous gullies. There are also some impressively bluffed valleys, most of them old lava flows eroded by water.

Where the elements allow, there are large areas of alpine herbfields and subalpine plants. The average elevation of the track is around 1400 metres, making it a harsh environment for both plants and trampers in bad weather, even during summer. Amongst others, the alpine plants include *Dracophyllum recurvum*, red tussock, snowberries, gentians, a buttercup and several species of daisy. One of these, the white daisy (*Celmisia incana*), is particularly prevalent, often forming large, uniform mats.

There are good views to Hauhungatahi, an old extinct volcano with partially forested flanks lying to the west. But the view that still draws your gaze most often is of the ever-dominant Mt Ruapehu, at 2797 metres the North Island's highest peak and New Zealand's loftiest volcano. The mountain also sports the most northerly glaciers in the country and the only ones in the North Island. In summer, two of these – the Mangaturuturu and Mangaehuehu – are clearly visible from this aspect.

Two streams that could prove difficult to ford when in flood are the Manganui o te Ao and Makatote rivers. The last watercourse crossed before Whakapapaiti Hut is the Whakapapaiti Stream. At the crossing point, a waterfall is clearly visible upstream, one of many that cascade over volcanic cliffs on the mountain flanks. A short distance beyond, you reach a track junction. Head left towards Whakapapaiti Hut (the right-hand branch is a possible exit route, ending at Bruce Road after one-and-a-half hours).

It's just 20 minutes from the junction to Whakapapaiti Hut, a large cabin set in a sheltered spot on the edge of the bushline. From here, the final day is a short one of only three hours or so, on a pleasantly untaxing section of track that largely passes through forest. A short distance down the valley from the hut, you cross the Whakapapaiti Stream and follow its true left bank for 45 minutes to the Mangahuia Track turnoff. Past here, the track crosses the Whakapapaiti Stream on a large wooden footbridge, then begins a sidle through groves of pahautea and cabbage trees mixed with beech forest, crossing a couple of gullies en route. The last section joins the Silica Rapids Track, a high-quality day track. Sections of boardwalk across sensitive moorlands give a last glimpse of Mt Ruapehu, and the first of Mt Ngauruhoe. Finally, there's one last stretch of forest before you emerge at Whakapapa Village.

Trampers cross a stream between Mangaturuturu and Whakapapaiti huts

Tama Lakes & Waihohonu

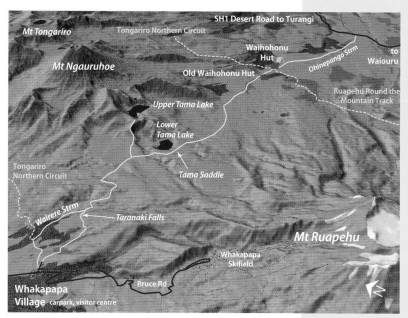

Duration 2 days

Grade Medium

Times Roadend to Tama Saddle: 2-2.5 hours. Side trip to Lower Tama Lake: 20 minutes return. Side trip to Upper Tama Lake: 1.5 hours return. Tama Saddle to Waihohonu Hut (29 bunks, gas heater and cooking rings, $25/night): 2.5–3 hours. Waihohonu Hut to Desert Road: 1.5–2 hours. Note that Waihohonu Hut is very popular and requires a dated Great Walks hut pass during the peak season between1 October and 30 April. During the off-peak season the hut does not have gas heating or cooking facilities and costs $15/night. A campsite exists near the hut and costs $20/night (off-peak $5/night).

Maps T19 Tongariro, T20 Ruapehu, Tongariro Parkmap

Access From SH 4 turn off at National Park and follow SH 47 for 10 km to where the signposted SH 48 branches off to Whakapapa Village. At the Whakapapa visitor centre there's a carpark, toilets and information. The signposted track to Taranaki Falls starts from nearby Ngauruhoe Place.

Alternative Route The Tongariro Northern Circuit Great Walk combines the Tama Lakes tramp with the Tongariro Alpine Crossing. Very fit trampers could accomplish this in a weekend, but most would want a more leisurely 3–4 days.

Information DOC Ruapehu Area Office, Ph 07 892 3729

The Tama Lakes, two sizeable sky-blue alpine lakes, lie in deep craters amongst the sharply etched volcanic landscape between Mts Ngauruhoe and Ruapehu. From Whakapapa, this two-day tramp leads eastward past the Taranaki Falls to Tama Saddle, where short side trips lead to the lakes, then beyond to the Waihohonu Hut on the eastern side of the park, and is part of the Tongariro Northern Circuit Great Walk. While crossing fairly gentle terrain, the route is very exposed to wind, snow and rain, and in poor visibility route-finding could be difficult.

From Whakapapa Village, a well-graded and gravelled track leads across alpine tussock and shrublands towards Taranaki Falls (an alternative lower route also leads to the falls, passing largely through beech forest). After about an hour you cross a footbridge over the Wairere Stream, just above Taranaki Falls. Shortly after, a track branches off, leading down a set of stairs to the base of the falls. Here, the Wairere River plunges 20 metres over a steep escarpment created by an old lava flow. The bluff overhangs, enabling those who don't mind a dousing to creep behind the falls and enjoy an unusual perspective of them.

Back at the track junction, head east on the track leading towards Waihohonu Hut. The route follows marker poles across an increasingly barren landscape towards Tama Saddle, the low point between Mts Ngauruhoe and Ruapehu. Both volcanoes are seen to good advantage, the classic steep-sided cone of Mt Ngauruhoe contrasting with the more angular form of Mt Ruapehu, here with the profile of an upturned shipwreck. In summer, this open expanse of country can be blisteringly hot, while in winter, snow often lies thickly over the area. Closer to the Tama Saddle, the volcanic soils are draped with circular clumps of the lime-green moss *Racomitrium lanuginosum*, testimony to the power of these primitive plants to cope with climatic extremes.

Tama Lakes and Mt Ruapehu, Tongariro National Park. (Photo: Darryn Pegram/Black Robin Photography)

An hour or two after Taranaki Falls, a signposted track branches off to the north, leading to the Upper Tama Lake. The complex topography here is a reminder that both present and past landscapes are very dynamic. Some 275,000 years ago there were probably andesitic volcanoes similar to Mt Ngauruhoe near where the Tama Lakes lie today. The ridge systems surrounding the lakes are remnants of these volcanoes, now shaved down by erosion to their very bases.

In contrast, the explosion craters filled by both Tama Lakes are much more recent. Upper Tama Lake lies close to the base of Mt Ngauruhoe and is the deeper and larger of the two. On a clear day, the ridge overlooking the lake makes a good spot to have some lunch and soak in the views. On such days when visibility is good, it is possible to loop back to the main track past the Lower Tama Lake.

Beyond the Tama Saddle, the high point of the track, a long and gradual descent marked by poles ensues into the Waihohonu Valley. Some distance to the east, the strikingly different fault topography of the Kaimanawa Range becomes apparent.

Streams radiating from Mt Ruapehu have carved the landscape into features that from aerial photographs resemble the slender toes of a giant creature. Even at ground level there's ample evidence of how easily water shapes such soft volcanic soils, and it's a wonder that plants survive here at all, where fragility and harshness mix in equal measure. As you lose altitude, however, the plants begin to gain a stronger hold once again. By the time subalpine shrubs appear, you've neared the end of the day's travel.

First though, is a worthwhile short visit to the historic Old Waihohonu Hut, the oldest-surviving hut in the park and, indeed, one of the more venerable back-country huts in New Zealand. It was built in 1903–04, as a stopover for stagecoaches travelling the

Desert Road between Pipiriki and Turangi. Later, the hut became a popular base for early travellers wanting to climb and ski on Mt Ruapehu. In 1997, major restoration work was carried out on the hut, which should ensure it lasts for several decades more – providing people respect the fact that it is no longer available for overnight accommodation. Interestingly, the walls have pumice for insulation, sandwiched between double layers of iron – a fascinating example of original Kiwi back-country architecture.

The new hut lies about 30 minutes away, down-valley and across on the true left of the Waihohonu River. Like all the huts on the Tongariro Northern Circuit, it can be very popular, so be aware of this particularly during holiday periods. On a fine morning it's worth the effort to rise early and watch the dawn sun illuminate Mt Ruapehu. Even from here, the mountain has a certain bulk to it, the sort of size that would make it still impressive if it was uplifted and deposited amongst the peaks of the Southern Alps.

For those returning to Whakapapa, it's a matter of retracing the previous day's footsteps, while for those who've made suitable travel arrangements, a shorter stroll leads out to the Desert Road. The latter track leads across more subalpine shrublands following the old Waihohonu coach road, through a section of forest and over the Ohinepango Stream via a footbridge, to end at the road.

Dawn over Mt Ruapehu and Waihohonu Valley

Bog Inn & Pureora

Duration 2 days

Grade Easy–Medium

Times Roadend to Bog Inn (4 bunks, woodstove, $5/night): 30–40 minutes. Bog Inn to Mt Pureora: 4 hours return.

Maps T18 Kuratau, T17 Whakamaru

Access From the Western Bays Road (SH 32), between Taupo and Turangi, turn onto Kakaho Road. Turn left onto Tihoi Road some 200 metres past the Kakaho camping area. Mill Road branches off to the left after 7 km, then forks into Bog Inn Road after a further 1.5 km.

Alternative Route From the top of Mt Pureora, you can follow a marked track over to Link Road, but this will require some transport juggling.

Information DOC Maniapoto Area Office, Ph 07 878 1050

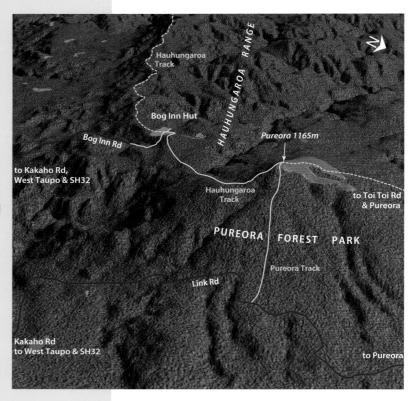

Pureora is one of a series of andesitic volcanoes in the central North Island that includes the more well-known mountains of Tongariro National Park. Pureora (the highest peak in Pureora Forest Park) and its neighbour, Titiraupenga, are now both extinct but form distinctive landmarks in the country west of Lake Taupo. Although Pureora is easily accessible on a day walk from Link Road near Pureora village, the tramp described here instead approaches the mountain from the south, linking it with an interesting wetland and a rustic hut called Bog Inn. Altogether, the tramp proves noteworthy for its plant diversity and for the outstanding views from Pureora's summit.

A washout has prematurely cut off vehicle access to the end of Bog Inn Road, and it is necessary to park your car and walk for 15 minutes to the start of the track. At the roadend the track crosses a small footbridge to where the signposted track enters the bush. After a 10-minute climb through dense forest, notable for the profusion of ferns and mosses, the track reaches the signposted Hauhungaroa Track where you head right.

The track now levels out and edges around an extensive wetland to another track junction. The Pureora Track heads right, while a five-minute track leads left to Bog Inn. The rather insalubriously named hut is indeed rustic but has considerable character: it was built from Hall's totara hacked from the nearby forest in 1960. Informal tracks lead into the nearby bog – a striking mosaic of vegetation that includes jointed rush, various sedges, *Gleichenia* ferns and sphagnum moss. Avoid wandering beyond the edge of the bog, as it's a very fragile environment and, unsurprisingly, often wet.

From Bog Inn there are views of your next destination, Pureora, lying to the north. From Bog Inn tramp for five minutes to the Hauhungaroa Track. You follow part of this 45-kilometre-long track to reach the summit of Pureora. Although it climbs steadily, the walk is never very strenuous, and changes in the forest with the increasing altitude prove interesting. At first there's podocarp forest dominated by Hall's totara and some huge fuchsia trees, the latter with orange bark peeling off in strips.

Higher up, the vegetation changes to 'goblin forest', consisting of kamahi, *Quintinia* and more Hall's totara. The track is rutted in places and can be slippery after rain or during winter, but it's not unduly taxing. Increasingly stunted forest – now including bog pine, broadleaf and a couple of *Olearia* species – signals that the summit is near, and you soon pop out onto a scrap of subalpine herbfield (a rarity in the King Country) where there is a small clearing and a summit trig.

Although from a distance Pureora (1165 m) appears to be a flattened, rather unimpressive cone, and considerably less spectacular than neighbouring Titiraupenga, its summit does provide a superb panorama of the Central North Island. To the south-east lies the expanse of Lake Taupo, flanked by the

Crown fern and podocarp forest, Pureora Forest Park

volcanoes of Mts Tongariro, Ngauruhoe and Ruapehu, neatly forming a line of vulcanism to remind you of Pureora's origins. On a clear day you might also see Mt Taranaki far to the southwest, while surrounding you are the extensive forests of Pureora itself. The 78,000-hectare Pureora Forest Park, created in 1978, is actually larger than many of the better-known tramping parks, including the Kaweka, Kaimanawa and Whirinaki forest parks. Despite Pureora's low summit, its exposed nature can make it a bleak place in bad weather, and occasional winter snowfalls are not unknown.

If you've made suitable transport arrangements, you can continue to traverse the mountain northwards on the Link Track (largely stepped and boardwalked), which leads down to Link Road (there's also another alternative track that leads down to Toi Toi Road). Otherwise, it's a plod back to Bog Inn and the walk out.

Waihaha Hut

Duration 1–2 days

Grade Easy

Time Carpark to Waihaha Hut (10 bunks, wood stove, $5/night): 3–4 hours

Map T18 Kuratau

Access The Waihaha Track starts beside the road bridge over the Waihaha River on the Western Bays Road (SH32) between Taupo and Turangi. It's clearly signposted, and there's a carpark on the opposite side of the road.

Alternative Route From Waihaha Hut, it's possible to follow the Hauhungaroa Track north as far as the Mangatu River (where there's a good campsite), and then tramp down the Mangatu River to its interception with the Waihaha Track. This does, however, require good river-crossing skills and fine weather.

Information DOC Maniapoto Area Office, Ph 07 878 1050

This track in the Pureora Forest Park follows the attractive Waihaha River through a succession of different forest types and ends at the very comfortable Waihaha Hut. Excellent birdlife is often encountered on the benched, all-weather track. As the height gain from start to finish is barely 100 metres, it makes a good destination for families or for the less physically fit.

From the Western Bays Road, the track immediately enters a section of low forest. The area is dominated by stands of golden-green celery pine (tanekaha), which lend it a brighter appearance than the more usual sombre forest tone. Initially, the track closely hugs the true left bank of the deep and slow-moving Waihaha River, with some views of outcrops of ignimbrite, a fine grained volcanic rock, on the far bank. Further up there's a brief but impressive gorge. Above the gorge, the river meanders over mossy rock ledges.

There's virtually no change in gradient until you cross a footbridge over the Mangatu River, a sizeable tributary of the Waihaha. On the far side, a steady but not very steep climb ensues up onto a terrace. En route are a couple of viewpoints from where you can glimpse the edge of Lake Taupo and the central volcanoes lying to the east. The eruption of Taupo more than 1800 years ago had a cataclysmic effect on Pureora, laying vast tracts of forest to waste. Although the podocarps that existed then now reign again, the composition of the forest has changed somewhat and is now largely without beech, except for a few isolated patches, one of them in the Mangatu valley.

Once you've gained the terrace, the track levels out again and soon emerges from the forest into the shrublands of the Pokiara Clearing. This fire-induced shrubland has been maintained by its openness to frosts, which have retarded invasion by forest species. There's a huge diversity of plants here, dominated by the rust-coloured monoao *Dracophyllum subulatum*. Closer inspection reveals a multitude of ferns, lichens and *Lycopodium* mosses, the latter appearing like miniature gold-coloured trees. In fact, the vegetation presents a subtle palette of varying shades, made even more colourful during the summer when many species are in flower.

Further along you get a glimpse of an impressive gorge through which the Waihaha River plunges. Aeons of erosion have carved great scalloped holes in the ignimbrite, forming a place to marvel at the artistry of water.

Not long after the gorge, the track passes into increasingly mature forest, dominated by rimu and matai above a canopy of tawa, and with large wheki-ponga in the understorey; their enormous skirts seemingly mimic those from the Victorian age. Pureora does not have such exquisitely dense stands of podocarps as those in Whirinaki, but they are

Podocarp forest, Waihaha valley, Pureora Forest Park

impressive nonetheless, and were similarly saved from logging only after a long battle by conservationists in the 1970s. The endangered blue-wattled kokako was the symbol of that fight, and although none exist in the Waihaha Valley, there is a good population in the northern blocks of Pureora. Despite the absence of kokako here, you are likely to hear a heartening number of birds, including kaka, kakariki, fantails, North Island robins, tomtits, grey warblers, kereru, whitehead and tui – partially a tribute to ongoing possum control in the area.

Quite suddenly, you emerge from the dark depths of the forest into a small clearing, the edge of which is occupied by Waihaha Hut. This modern hut, with a spacious interior and large veranda, was opened in March 2001 after its predecessor burnt down the year before. It's a great place to enjoy the simplicity of hut life: boil the billy, cook your evening meal and perhaps retire to the veranda to listen to the evening chorus.

Along with Bog Inn, Waihaha Hut is one of three huts linking a tramping route over the Hauhungaroa Range. If you have the time and energy, you can make a short excursion along part of this track either to the north or south. The southern route is flatter and offers chances to spy blue duck in the river.

The diversity of plant communities on the walk out more than compensates for the fact that you have to retrace your footsteps, and it also gives you another chance to hear the secretive fernbirds that live in the Pokiara Clearing.

Gorge, Waihaha River

Waipakihi Hut

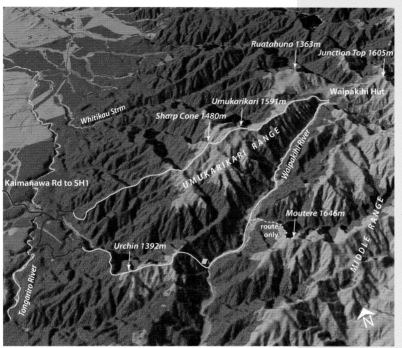

Duration 2–3 days

Grade Medium

Times Roadend to Waipakihi Hut (12 bunks, woodstove, $5/night) via Umukarikari Range: 4–6 hours. Waipakihi Hut to roadend via Waipakihi River and Urchin: 6–8 hours.

Maps T19 Tongariro, Kaimanawa Forest Parkmap

Access Turn left off SH1, 15 km south of Turangi onto Kaimanawa Road. After 4 km turn left onto a side road marked with a sign to the Umukarikari Track, which immediately crosses a bridge over a stream. After 500 m take a right and follow this road to the end, where there is space to park and a signpost to the track. The tramp ends on another road nearby (5 km away), so you will either have to walk back to your car or arrange a lift.

Alternative Route From Waipakihi Hut it's possible to traverse the Middle Range as far as Thunderbolt and then drop down to the river on an unmaintained route from Motutere. This would require at least an extra day, and as the route traverses some blocks of private land (in the vicinity of Junction Top) a permit must be obtained from the landowner prior to entering the area. Permits for access to these blocks are available from Air Charter Taupo, 07 378 5467.

Information DOC Turangi–Taupo Area Office, Ph 07 386 8607

While it is undoubtedly overshadowed by the attractions of the adjacent Tongariro National Park, the Kaimanawa Range does offer some good tramping. One of the most popular overnight trips in the park is the walk over the Umukarikari Range to Waipakihi Hut. The second day involves ambling down the Waipakihi River, followed by a sharp, not-so-short climb over a peak called Urchin. Altogether this tramp makes the ideal introduction to Kaimanawa tramping and forms one of the park's few round trips that can be accomplished in a weekend.

From some viewpoints the Waipakihi Valley looks like it should be in the South Island: broad tussock flats lie expansively below beech-clad spurs that rise to substantial tops.

However, chattering whiteheads on the walk in will soon dispel any illusions that you are anywhere but in the North Island. After an initially flattish walk

Mts Ruapehu and Ngauruhoe from Middle Range

through beech forest, the track begins a steady climb onto a broad spur that you ascend for some 3 kilometres onto the Umukarikari Range.

While in places there are some alpine plants – notably tussock, *Dracophyllum recurvum*, *Celmisia spectabilis* and bluebells – the Umukarikari is typical of many broad Kaimanawa tops in that it has scant vegetation and few or no tarns. By this stage the good views westwards towards Mts Ruapehu, Ngauruhoe and Tongariro further remind you that you are firmly in the volcanic interior of the North Island. Indeed, ash and pumice deposits from previous eruptions, particularly the massive Taupo eruption of 186 AD, are plainly obvious in Kaimanawa soils and sometimes lie several metres deep.

The Umukarikari tops prove so rolling that they almost disguise the fact you are climbing, following a poled route over Sharp Cone and onto the high point of Umukarikari (1591 m). From here, the Waipakihi Valley stretches out before you, while further east are the seemingly endless ridges of the Kaimanawa ranges and beyond, those of the Kawekas. Under heavy winter snow, the Umukarikari tops have good potential for cross-country skiing – of course, only after you have lugged your skis up! On a bleak day, however, travel along the range can be something of a slog as there's no shelter and you're exposed to weather from almost every direction.

The descent into the head of the Waipakihi River (where the hut is situated) proves as undulating as the ascent. The final section passes through subalpine scrub, crosses a small side stream and then climbs up to a bench where the 12-bunk hut lies. This can be a popular spot on summer weekends, but if the hut is full there are plenty of spots in which to camp nearby.

Alternatively, on a hot day there are ample spots in which to camp downstream. During summer the walk down the Waipakihi River is pure delight. There are easy tussock flats for most of the way, ample swimming and, if the sun gets too much, plenty of sheltered beech enclaves where you can retire to the shade. Indeed, a recent DOC study found that the river flats of the Waipakihi Valley are 'Arguably the best area of riparian tussock grasslands remaining in the North Island.' Be warned, though, that numerous river crossings are required, and after heavy rain it would be best instead to exit back over the Umukarikari Range.

From Waipakihi Hut it takes about four to five hours to reach a signposted track leading up to Urchin (1392 m), a tussock-covered knoll overlooking the middle reaches of the river. Nearby is a very good campsite for those who prefer to stretch the tramp over three days. The route up Urchin makes no detours: it climbs right from the start and keeps doing so until you reach the bushline some 300 vertical metres later. Your reward is excellent views over the valley.

A poled route leads for 2 kilometres over the tops of Urchin, then the final part of the tramp descends through beech forest to a carpark on a branch of Kaimanawa Road. The forest understorey is surprisingly lush here, with mosses, liverworts and various *Blechnum* ferns.

Waipakihi River, Kaimanawa Forest Park

Kaipo River

Duration 2–3 days

Grade Medium

Times Clements Mill Road to Tiki Tiki Stream: 4–5 hours. Tiki Tiki Stream to Cascade Hut (6 bunks, wood stove, $5/night) via Kaipo River and Kaipo Saddle: 5–7 hours. Cascade Hut to Clements Mill Road: 4–6 hours.

Map U19 Kaimanawa

Access Turn off SH 5 (the Napier–Taupo Road) 27 km from Taupo onto Taharua Road, and follow this for 9 km before turning onto Clements Mill Road. Follow Clements Mill Road for 5 km until reaching the Te Iringa Track carpark. The tramp ends at a second carpark a further 16 km along Clements Mill Road, which will require a car juggle, or a long road walk.

Alternative Route From Cascade Hut, trampers can walk out to Kiko Road via Ngapuketurua (6–9 hours). Note that rain can make the Tauranga–Taupo River impossible to ford, and the tops over Ngapuketurua are exposed and sparsely marked. Between Cascade Hut and Ngapuketurua the route crosses private land, requiring a permit from Air Charter Taupo ($25 per person). Ph 07 378 5467, info@airchartertaupo.co.nz

Information DOC Turangi – Taupo Area Office, Ph 07 386 8607

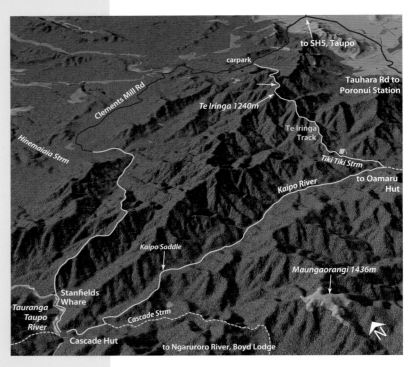

This pleasant round trip in the northern part of Kaimanawa Forest Park arcs through some of the most attractive beech forests in the North Island. The route uses good tracks in the headwaters of both the Kaipo and Tauranga–Taupo catchments, and has two huts plus a number of excellent places to camp.

In 1982 Cyclone Bernie played havoc with the area, devastating whole sections of forests and obliterating many tracks. For many years the route up the Kaipo was marked but not maintained, requiring considerable effort to clamber over extensive windfall in the headwaters. However DOC has recently re-cut the track, making a weekend trip a possibility once again.

Over three days the logical sequence involves camping one night beside Tiki Tiki Stream and spending the second night at Cascade Hut. Completing the tramp over two days will require one very long day, or perhaps two moderate days with a camp somewhere in the Kaipo headwaters. Be aware that the area is extremely popular with hunters, and probably best avoided during the Roar (late March and early April).

From the carpark, the benched Te Iringa track ascends at a suitably pleasant angle through some exquisite stands of red beech forest. Occasional clumps of mountain cabbage trees add diversity to the forest, their broad, long leaves contrasting strongly with the more delicate beech foliage.

The track boasts the sort of easy gradient that leaves enough lung capacity for a sociable chat with your companions. That is surely one of the great aspects of tramping: the opportunity to spend a number of days with friends, not just a couple of hours over a latte in a café.

Higher up, the track passes the site of the old Te Iringa Hut, burnt down some years ago. After sidling east of Te Iringa (1240 m), the track follows broad forested ridges for some distance before beginning a gentle descent into Tiki Tiki Stream. Beside a fork in the stream, the track reaches a good, well-used camping area.

Beyond, the track meanders on the true left bank of the Tiki Tiki Stream until reaching a swingbridge over the Kaipo River. At the track junction on the far bank, head up the Kaipo Valley (the other branch leads to Oamaru Hut). The Kaipo River is a sizeable watercourse draining this forested northeastern part of Kaimanawa Forest Park, and the lower reaches contain some delightful sections of stout red beech, their trunks moss- and lichen-encrusted.

Junction of Tiki Tiki Stream and Kaipo River, Kaimanawa Forest Park

The merging of Tiki Tiki Stream and the Kaipo makes a picturesque scene. Beech trees lean over the river to clasp each other like old relatives, the stream spills over a wide rapid, and the cool, green waters flow over submerged boulders of a reddish hue.

Shortly upstream of the Tiki Tiki junction, the track passes the Kaipo's most significant rapid, where water rushes through a jumble of rough-hewn ignimbrite boulders. Pumice and ignimbrite are recurring geological themes in this part of the world, one as soft a rock as you can imagine and the other considerably more resilient.

The track, well marked by plastic orange triangles, follows the river terraces in places and the riverbed in others, at first staying largely on the true right. It's quite a long way up-valley, and the size of the river diminishes only slowly. Eventually, near the Kaipo headwaters, the river finally narrows. Where it dwindles to creek size at a prominent fork, the track leaves the river and begins a climb up a forested spur to Kaipo Saddle.

From Kaipo Saddle, a good open track descends through forest down a defined ridge into Cascade Stream, which is forded to reach a signposted track junction. Ignore the track which branches off to the North Arm and Boyd Lodge, and continue down the valley.

Cascade Stream takes its name from an exquisite rapid which has grooved and sculpted its way through ignimbrite boulders. It's about a 30-minute tramp down-valley on the true left to Cascade Hut, which is located just upstream of the Tauranga–Taupo River.

The track out to Clements Mill Road crosses Cascade Stream just downstream of the hut, then follows a flat, wide section of track through several clearings, down the true right bank of the Tauranga–Taupo River. If river levels allow, it's worth fording across to Stanfield's Whare, an historic hut visible on the true left bank, about 20 minutes from Cascade Hut.

Built in 1958 from beech poles and a malthoid roof, Stanfield's Whare still remains dry and habitable thanks to maintenance by locals who care about the place. Its chimney, constructed out of pumice stones, reputedly leaks smoke out of every crevice. Inside there are two bunks that don't look very level, and stuffed into every available space is the sort of hut detritus – tins, can openers, bottles – that always accumulates over the years. It has loads of character, and is far from being 'derelict', as marked on old maps.

Back on the true right, the track continues along flats beside the Tauranga–Taupo for another 15 minutes before beginning a solid 460-metre climb up a forested ridge to its crest at 1240 metres. Then it's down, down, along the northern side of the ridge into more undulating terrain in the headwaters of the Hinemaiaia Stream. From here the track largely follows the Hinemaiaia Stream on the true left until shortly before reaching the roadend.

Tarawera Falls– Lake Okataina

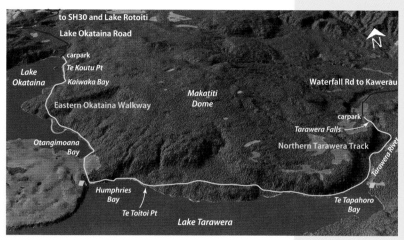

to SH30 and Lake Rotoiti
Lake Okataina Road
carpark
Te Koutu Pt
Lake Okataina
Kaiwaka Bay
Waterfall Rd to Kawerau
Makatiti Dome
Eastern Okataina Walkway
carpark
Tarawera Falls
Otangimoana Bay
Northern Tarawera Track
Tarawera River
Humphries Bay
Te Tapahoro Bay
Te Toitoi Pt
Lake Tarawera
N

Duration 2 days

Grade Easy

Times Tarawera Falls Carpark to Te Tapahoro Bay: 1.5–2 hours. Te Tapahoro Bay to Humphries Bay: 3 hours. Humphries Bay to Lake Okataina Road: 2.5–3 hours.

Map V16 Tarawera

Access to Tarawera Falls Road access to Tarawera Falls lies through a private plantation forest reached from Kawerau, and a permit must be obtained from the Visitor Information Centre (Ph 07 323 7550) on the day of your intended trip. Permits cost $3.50 per vehicle. From Kawerau, turn off Tamarangi Drive into Islington Street, then right onto Onslow Street, left onto Fenton Street, right onto River Road and left onto Waterhouse Street. From there private forest roads are followed: Tarawera Road, Fenton Mill Road and finally turn left onto Waterfall Road. In total it is 25 km from Kawerau or 30 minutes drive, mainly on gravel roads.

Access to Lake Okataina The tramp ends at Lake Okataina, at the end of Lake Okataina Road which branches off SH 30, approximately 20 km from Rotorua. The 6-km road ends at a carpark where there is a lodge, picnic area, toilets, shelter, information panels and jetty.

Boat Access The camping areas at Te Tapahoro and Humphries bays can be accessed by boat or sea kayak on Lake Tarawera.

Information DOC Rotorua, Ph 07 366 1080

Rotorua does not have a significant national park or forest park nearby (perhaps it should) but the area instead boasts a number of sizeable scenic reserves, many of them contiguous with each other. By linking tracks through the Tarawera Falls, Lake Tarawera and Lake Okataina scenic reserves trampers can complete a very enjoyable tramp, with a night spent camping at Humphries Bay en route. Transport is somewhat difficult to arrange, and will probably require a drop-off and pick-up at either end.

From the Tarawera Falls carpark, a well-developed, easy walking track leads upstream on the true right of the Tarawera River for 10 minutes before crossing a footbridge to the true left. Another 10 minutes walk upstream leads to a viewing area of the 65-metre Tarawera Falls.

Tarawera Falls erupt from a fissure in an impressive rhyolite cliff, an explosion of water that is perhaps unique in New Zealand, certainly in the Bay of Plenty. The cliffs themselves resulted after a rhyolitic lava flow from nearby Mt Tarawera some 11,000 years ago abruptly ended. Adding interest to the area is the unusual mixture of rata and pohutukawa, the

Sunset at Lake Okataina Scenic Reserve, Rotorua

latter normally associated with coastal areas. The two *Metrosideros* species have interbred to produce hybrid specimens with varying leaf shapes.

From the falls, take the Northern Tarawera Track which heads towards Lake Tarawera.

The track climbs stiffly at first to reach a point above the falls. Here, a signposted track junction offers a shortcut that will save 10 minutes walking; but the more scenic option is to take a track that follows the Tarawera River. On this latter track, dazzlingly clear blue pools alternate between cascades and tranquil pools, and at one point the entire river boils into an underground passage.

The wide, easy track remains on the true left of the river all the way to Te Tapahoro Bay, passing through sections of manuka and rata forest, all regenerated since the mighty Tarawera eruption of 1886. In places moss and fern make delightful mosaics on the forest floor. Shortly before the track reaches the lake, the valley opens out and passes a raupo wetland.

Where the Tarawera River issues from the voluminous Lake Tarawera, a wooden footbridge leads across to a popular campsite at Te Tapahoro Bay (which is also accessible by boat or road). It is worth continuing on for another five minutes along the Northern Tarawera Track to a jetty offering fine views over the lake with Mt Tarawera brooding above. It makes a great lunch stop.

Beyond the jetty, the Northern Tarawera Track largely hugs the shoreline, and remains wide and well benched. An hour after leaving Te Tapahoro Bay, the track skirts up an enclosed gully, and climbs up to a flat forested terrace well back from the lake. This undulating terrain makes for easy tramping, and after 90 minutes reaches the lake once again at Te Toitoi Point after a short descent. Humphries Bay lies 30 minutes around the lakeshore. The Northern Tarawera Track ends here.

Happily, the small camping area at Humphries Bay (toilets available) is reserved for overnight trampers or kayakers – not boaties. Overlooking Lake Tarawera towards Mt Tarawera, the bay is often a peaceful spot, although it is exposed to southerly gales.

After a night camped at Humphries Bay, you begin on the Eastern Okataina Walkway. The walkway at first strikes inland over the narrow isthmus separating Lakes Tarawera and Okataina. This is an easy, gentle ascent on a good track, taking only 20–25 minutes, but imagine Maori warriors hauling waka carved from trees over here! In times past Lake Okataina was part of an important transport waterway used by local Maori that connected Lake Rotoiti with Tarawera.

The track reaches Lake Okataina at Otangimoana Bay, providing a pleasant place to rest and have a snack. Of all Rotorua's numerous lakes, Okataina is arguably the most attractive; certainly the one in most pristine condition. The deep lake was formerly an arm of Lake Tarawera, until a lava dome erupted about 7000 years ago in the vicinity of what is now Humphries Bay, thereby separating the two.

Beyond Otangimoana Bay, the track skirts slopes above the lake's eastern shore, following 'walkway' posts about 10 metres above lake level. After 30 minutes walk, the track strikes inland. Undulating travel leads through forest dominated by rewarewa, mahoe, kamahi, tawa and rata, with silver fern conspicuous in the understorey. After an hour in this dense forest, you reach the lake once again at Kaiwaka Bay. Te Kouto Point, a mound-shaped peninsula that has an uncanny similarity to the toe of a steel-capped boot, is clearly visible to the north. It takes 30–40 minutes to tramp along the lake edge until a signpost indicates the five-minute side trail that branches off onto the peninsula.

The side track ends at a small south-facing bay on the peninsula, near the historic Te Kouto Pa site. Ngati Tarawhai, a sub-tribe of Te Arawa, established their main pa here, and lived in the area for centuries before abandoning it some time prior to 1900. Their reasons for departure are interesting: Lake Okataina has no natural outlet, and instead drains into Lake Tarawera (which is 20 metres lower in elevation) by seeping through lava below Otangimoana Bay. Naturally, such a slow drainage mechanism ensures the level of Lake Okataina rises and falls quite dramatically, according to rainfall. For example, between 1962 and 1971 the lake level rose 3 metres, and as a consequence drowned beaches and submerged forest. For Ngati Tarawhai, these irregular fluctuations ultimately proved too difficult to live with.

In 1921, through an act of considerable generosity, Ngati Tarawhai gifted the lake shores to the Crown, forming the basis for the Lake Okataina Scenic Reserve. The magnitude of such a gift, similar to that which led to the formation of Tongariro National Park, is quite staggering when you consider all that Maori suffered during European colonisation. Given how much native forest was converted to pine forest in the Bay of Plenty during later decades, trampers can be grateful that the reserve was established.

Past Te Kouto Point, the main walkway passes a large natural amphitheatre known as the Soundshell, then follows close to the lake shore until reaching the carpark at Lake Okataina Road. Some excellent information panels detail the area's history, and a nearby shelter offers respite from sun or rain. Altogether the diverse landscapes, interesting history and scenic bush makes this an enjoyable, easy trip, even if the tramping lacks much challenge.

Central Whirinaki Hut

WHIRINAKI FOREST PARK

Duration 2–3 days

Grade Medium

Times Road to Mangamate Hut (9 bunks, woodstove, $5/night): 3.5–4 hours. Mangamate to Central Whirinaki Hut (24 bunks, woodstove, $15/night): 5–6 hours. Central Whirinaki Hut to road: 4–6 hours

Map V18 Whirinaki

Access Access is from State Highway 38, 18 km east of Murupara, where a signposted turn-off directs you towards the town of Minginui. Don't go into the town, but turn right across the bridge over the Whirinaki River, and then turn left onto River Road. About 1 km from the end of River Road there's a large carpark and a toilet. As vehicle break-ins can be a problem here, you may like to take advantage of the 'drop-off and pick-up' service provided by transport operators in nearby Minginui.

Alternative Routes To shorten the trip, you could just walk to Central Whirinaki Hut and return along the same route. Some people combine this trip with a visit to the Upper Whirinaki Hut (see page 113).

Information DOC Rangitaiki Area Office, Ph 07 366 1080

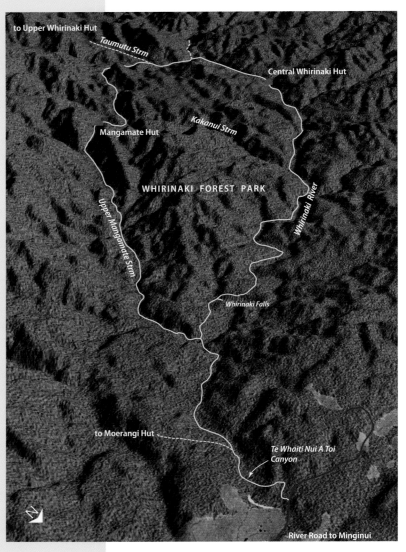

The track into Central Whirinaki is undoubtedly the most popular overnight tramp in Whirinaki Forest Park, and it certainly passes through some of the finest podocarp forest in the country. Superlatives often used to describe this forest include 'cathedral-like', 'dinosaur relic' and 'majestic'. The podocarp trees of Central Whirinaki certainly occur in a density rarely encountered elsewhere, and they form a unique glimpse into the type of forests that once dominated the ancient continent of Gondwana some 150 million years ago.

The track described here forms a convenient loop, combining two huts and both the Mangamate and Whirinaki valleys. From River Road, a well-benched and graded track leads through a magnificent section of forest dominated by podocarps. All five of the major podocarp species – rimu, kahikatea, miro, totara and matai – are present, and the forest really does exude a feeling of antiquity. You soon cross a footbridge which provides a good view of the Te Whaiti Nui A Toi Canyon, an ignimbrite slot gorge through which the sizeable Whirinaki River flows swiftly.

Rimu trees, Central Whirinaki

Upstream, the track follows terraces on the true right of the river, passing the turn-off to Moerangi Hut, crossing a second footbridge and then coming to yet another fork in the track. Head left here towards Mangamate Hut. This section of track is noticeably rougher and largely follows the course of the Upper Mangamate Stream with frequent river crossings. Watch out for the stinging nettle ongaonga (best avoided) and blue ducks (which will probably try to avoid you). An abundance of toetoe is a feature of many Whirinaki rivers, and the Mangamate is no exception – you'll be lucky to arrive at the hut without cuts.

Mangamate Hut was recently relocated to a sunnier and drier spot on a forested saddle at the head of Mangamate Stream. From the hut you drop briefly down into the Kakanui Stream, before surmounting another forested saddle into the Taumutu catchment. More stream travel ensues, through a magnificent stand of red beech trees, before you reach a track junction. Here, keep heading down the Taumutu Stream (unless you're planning to visit Upper Whirinaki Hut, which lies on the track heading upstream).

At the confluence of the Taumutu Stream and Whirinaki River, pass a track and footbridge leading off to the left and continue down the valley. The track is wide and well-benched once again, and the Central Whirinaki Hut is only a couple of kilometres away. This large and popular hut lacks the cosiness of the other smaller huts in the park, but you can escape any crowds by camping in one of the many spots in the surrounding flats.

Your final day, which follows a gentle track down the true right of the Whirinaki River, really is the highlight. The track's remarkably level gradient allows rapid progress, but it would be a shame to rush it, and you should allow plenty of time to admire the podocarps that often tower a neck-straining distance upwards into the canopy above.

The fact that Whirinaki can be enjoyed by trampers at all is due to the concerted and determined efforts of conservationists. Logging in the area began in 1928, and as recently as the 1970s and early 1980s the New Zealand Forest Service was still extracting timber. Lumber was then the mainstay of nearby Minginui. In the late 1970s, a group of prominent scientists – including the then Auckland University zoology professor John Morton and botany lecturer John Ogden – banded together with others in a determined effort to save the remaining forest from destruction. Morton called the forests of Whirinaki one of the most 'faithful representations of a Mesozoic plant community remaining on earth'. Their efforts finally precipitated the formation of the 55,000-hectare Whirinaki Forest Park in 1984. Together with Northland Forest Park, Whirinaki was the last of the forest parks created under the administration of the Forest Service, some three years prior to the formation of DOC.

There are many footbridges to cross en route, plus one short, five-minute side trip to view the Whirinaki Falls. Not far beyond the falls you finally meet the Mangamate Track junction once again. The round trip now complete, it's just an amble back past the canyon and across the river to the carpark.

Mangamate River

Upper Whirinaki Hut

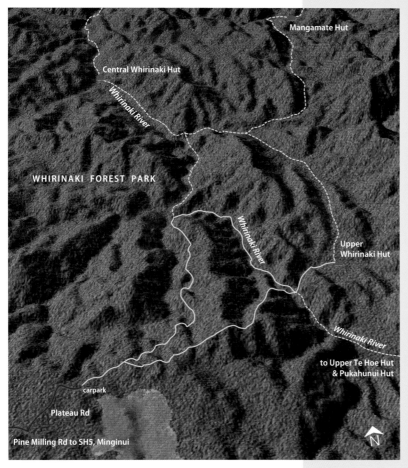

Duration 2 days

Grade Easy–Medium

Times Plateau Road to caves: 1.5–2 hours. Caves to Upper Whirinaki Hut (9 bunks, woodstove, $5/night): 2 hours. Upper Whirinaki Hut to Plateau Road via ridge track: 2.5–3 hours.

Map V18 Whirinaki

Access Access to Plateau Road is either through the Waipunga Valley (off SH 5 between Napier and Taupo) or through forestry roads accessible from Minginui. Direct access through Kaingaroa Forest from SH 38 is no longer possible. Make sure you have a good map for negotiating the potentially confusing myriad of roads to get there.

Alternative routes Some people combine a visit to Upper Whirinaki Hut with the tramp into Central Whirinaki. From Upper Whirinaki it is also possible to complete a longer tramp to Upper Te Hoe Hut and out via the Pukahunui Stream.

Information DOC Rangitaiki Area Office, Ph 07 366 1080

This is a less well-known but pleasant two-day tramp to Upper Whirinaki Hut, which lies in the southwestern corner of Whirinaki Forest Park. It's a fairly easy round trip, with undulating bush tracks, no major climbs and one section of river travel. Although it lacks the 'cathedral-like' podocarp groves of Central Whirinaki, the tramp is usually quieter and there are good opportunities to see blue duck in the river section.

From the carpark at the end of Plateau Road, a well-benched track winds its way around the spurs of a bush ridge towards the Whirinaki River. Beech forest dominates here, with occasional podocarps – mainly rimu – breaking the uniformity of the canopy.

Whirinaki River, Whirinaki Forest Park

Large mountain cabbage trees, or ti toi, frequently hang like umbrellas over the track. After a couple of hours you reach the main Whirinaki River at a footbridge. Nearby caves marked on the map are accessible as a short side trip from here, and the larger one harbours glow-worms. These are not true limestone caves but were formed as the stream excavated the highly erodable pumice deposits.

Once across the footbridge, you come to a track junction; head upstream (the other track leads to Central Whirinaki). The track now meanders, crossing the river in places that are mostly shallow and easily forded. There's nothing strenuous about travel up this attractive upper section of the Whirinaki River, but when it is in flood the trip would prove impossible. This easy tramping leaves plenty of energy to listen out for the kaka and kakariki, which are still relatively abundant in the area, or perhaps for contemplation of the surrounding topography.

Whirinaki is essentially a heavily dissected landscape lying between the plains of the Kaingaroa to the west and the fault mountains of Te Urewera National Park to the east. Covering the underlying ignimbrite and greywacke are layers of ash and pumice, and the latter is often seen in the river. During the 1995–96 Ruapehu eruptions, much of Whirinaki's forests were covered in a fine layer of ash. While the power of the volcano to emit ash over such distances is astonishing, these latest Ruapehu rumbles were but minor episodes in the area's long history of vulcanism. When Taupo last erupted around 186 AD, the Chinese noted the explosion, and it remains the largest known eruption in recorded history. This catastrophic event significantly affected the topography and vegetation of surrounding areas such as Whirinaki.

About 2 kilometres upstream of the swingbridge, you reach a prominent signposted four-way track junction. To the south, the track continues up-valley and eventually passes into the Te Hoe catchment. To the west lies your route out over a bush ridge back to Plateau Road, while to the east lies Upper Whirinaki Hut, now just a 20-minute amble away up a small tributary of the main river. The hut, tidy like all of those in the park, is situated at the far end of a grassy clearing with a prominent podocarp rising on the left. It has nine bunks and a woodstove – perfect for cold winter weekends.

On the final day, trace your route back to the track junction. Take the signposted track leading to Plateau Road, which climbs briskly up onto a bush ridge. While this is a rougher trail than the well-maintained and benched track of the first leg of the tramp, it offers a good way to complete the round trip.

Crown fern and red beech trees

Roger's (Te Wairoa) Hut

Duration 2 days

Grade Easy–Medium

Times Okahu roadend to Whangatawhia (Skips) Hut (9 bunks, wood stove, $5/night): 1.5–2 hours. Whangatawhia to Roger's Hut (6 bunks, wood stove, $5/night): 1.5 hours.

Map V18 Whirinaki

Access The Okahu Valley Road branches off SH 38 at Ngaputahi, about 25 km east of Murupara. The 13 km-long road ends at a parking area with toilets and picnic tables.

Alternative Route From Roger's Hut, trampers can follow the Moerangi River and track to Moerangi Hut (9 bunks, wood stove, $5/night), and then use the track that crosses Moerangi into the Whirinaki Valley. Allow an extra day. Local operators can arrange transport for this through trip.

Information DOC Murupara, Ph 07 366 1080

The appeal of many back-country huts lies in their spectacular locations. However others, like Roger's Hut in Whirinaki Forest Park, make a worthy destination simply for their own character and history.

Roger's Hut dates from just before the hut-building boom instigated by the New Zealand Forest Service in the mid 1950s, and its square design and slab construction contrast to the later NZFS huts. A Department of Internal Affairs team led by culler Rex Forrester built Rogers Hut in 1952, as part of the deer control operations that the agency had begun in 1930. During the first two decades, most cullers worked from semi-permanent tent camps because of the financial restrictions imposed first by the great Depression and then by World War II. By the 1950s, however, funds became available for more substantial accommodation in the form of huts.

Some of the huts from this era were built by cullers who lacked the necessary carpentry skills, so have not survived. Forrester, however, had learnt the art of hand-splitting timber with an axe, in the manner of many pioneer New Zealand buildings. The matai studs and red beech used in the construction of Rogers Hut were split on site, saving considerable

Roger's (Te Wairoa) Hut, Whirinaki Forest Park

effort and expense. Testimony to Forrester's skill is the fact that the hut – with a little ongoing maintenance – has lasted more than half a century.

Occupying a small clearing in the valley, the bright orange hut has changed little since the 1950s except for the replacement of the original flat iron roof with corrugated iron, and a veranda floor (added in 1995). With smoke creeping out the chimney, and mist closing in on the surrounding canopy, it is a place with considerable back-country atmosphere.

The easiest access to Roger's Hut is from the Okahu Valley, in the northeast of Whirinaki Forest Park, using a good benched track typical of the park. From the Okahu road end, the track wends slowly uphill, cresting a low bush saddle after about 25–30 minutes. From here, the track descends gradually into the Whangatawhia Valley, through forest dominated by beech but with the occasional rimu and kahikatea.

To reach Whangatawhia (Skips) Hut requires another hour or so of walking on the delightfully easy, all-weather track, which crosses several footbridges en route. Shortly before the hut, the track passes an attractive waterfall. Whangatawhia Hut, located in a small grassy clearing, has – like several others in Whirinaki Forest Park – three tiers of three bunks.

Beyond Whangatawhia Hut, the track continues southward, sidling high above the stream until it reaches another low saddle at 700 metres. There's a particularly fine stand of red beech here, and observant trampers might hear kaka overhead or spot North Island robins on the forest floor. As it shares a boundary with Te Urewera National Park, Whirinaki is part of the largest tract of forest in the North Island and consequently boasts good birdlife.

From the saddle, the track descends into the Whakangutuwhio Stream. While the track is easy going, it belies the tortuous nature of the terrain here; a crumpled landscape of confusing ridges overlaid with dense forest and little in the way of clearings. Maori warrior Te Kooti was a master at travelling through such difficult country, and he based himself in the area briefly during 1871. As the name of the Whakangutuwhio Stream suggests, whio (blue duck) live in the vicinity, and a pair can often be observed near Roger's Hut.

Beech forest, Whirinaki Forest Park

The hut itself occupies another grassy clearing, about five minutes beyond a large footbridge that spans the Moerangi Stream. Although sometimes called Te Wairoa Hut, the name 'Roger's' holds most sway. Rex Forrester named the hut after his son, Roger, who was born during its construction. Materials such as windows, iron and nails were brought in part way by pack-horse through the Waiau Valley, but the remaining terrain proved too rugged for hoofed traffic. Instead, Forrester and three others lugged loads on their own backs for the final section to the hut. Construction began in 1951, but it was not completed until the following year. The hut's original dirt floor was later replaced by the tongue and groove wooden floor of today, and a woodstove has superseded the open fire.

Forrester went on to become a well-known professional guide and author, writing hunting classics like *The Chopper Boys* and *The Helicopter Hunters*. He died in 2001. The following year, Roger Forrester scattered his father's ashes near the hut. For a man who spent so much of his life in the bush, there couldn't be a better resting place.

The role of huts as part of our back-country heritage is slowly becoming accepted, even celebrated. Indeed, the Department of Conservation has in recent years identified many huts worthy of historic status. Roger's, along with another hut also built by Forrester called Te Totara (in Te Urewera National Park), are among the few slab huts remaining in New Zealand from this era. However, as the use it still receives by trampers and hunters testifies, Roger's Hut is no museum piece. Surely that would have pleased Rex Forrester.

Te Puia Lodge

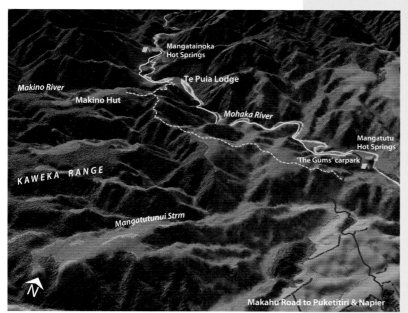

Duration 2 days

Grade Easy

Times Makahu Road to Te Puia Lodge (24 bunks, gas heater and cooking rings, $15/night): 2.5–3 hours. Te Puia to Mangatainoka Hot Springs: 30–40 minutes each way.

Maps U20 Kaweka, U19 Kaimanawa, Kaweka Forest Parkmap

Access From Napier drive 60 km to Puketitiri. The tarseal ends 4 km past Puketitiri. Shortly afterwards, the road forks. Turn right into Pakaututu Road and follow it for 9 km until turning left on Makahu Road for 10 km to reach 'The Gums' carpark. Two bridges now avoid fords, but it's a narrow windy road, and the entire drive from Napier takes 90 minutes or more.

Alternative Route From Te Puia Lodge, it's possible to complete a satisfying round trip back to Makahu Road via the Makino Hut and Makino Track (grade: medium).

Information DOC Hawke's Bay Area Office, Ph 06 834 3111

A large hut, a sizeable river with good swimming holes and hot pools at both the start and end of the tramp – what more could you ask for? This easy tramp in Kaweka Forest Park was made for a luxurious weekend, and the hot springs are a real treat, especially during the winter. From the Mangatutu Hot Springs, the track follows the Mohaka River to Te Puia Lodge, where a short diversion is possible up to the Mangatainoka Hot Springs.

'The Gums', a carpark and camping area at the end of Makahu Road, is reached only after a long and very winding drive inland from Napier. Once there, however, you do not need to shoulder your pack immediately. Some 500 metres back along the road, a five-minute walk leads to the well-developed Mangatutu Hot Springs, where an old fisheries tub is partially sunk into a wooden deck. There's room for four to five people, and a dip makes a very pleasant way to begin your tramp (note: keep your head above water to prevent any chance of contracting amoebic meningitis).

Local Maori were well familiar with the Mangatutu Hot Springs and had settlements near here and at the Mangatainoka Hot Springs, where they caught eels in the Mohaka.

Mohaka River, Kaweka Forest Park

The first Pakeha route, suitable for horse-drawn vehicles, came through in 1915 but soon deteriorated. Then, in 1962, the New Zealand Forest Service opened a road, although it was not until 1990 that access became possible by two-wheel drive.

Beware of soaking too long, or you'll reach such a state of torpor that even the two or three hour walk to Te Puia Lodge will seem just too much. From the carpark, the track climbs up and down for a short section before crossing a small creek and heading north onto some open flats beside the Mohaka River. The Mohaka is one of the principal rivers of the Kaweka Range and is a large body of water well-known for its good trout fishing and excellent rafting. The vegetation here is mostly regenerating following burning of the primary forest by early graziers and is at first dominated by kanuka and manuka. Both trees are eye-catching when in flower, when they sometimes give the appearance of being covered by a light sprinkling of snow.

After rounding a shoulder, the track heads westward again and along to a pleasant gravelly beach, where there is a large swimming hole and some river reflections. The next section of track has literally been carved out of the cliffside, a result of improvements made during the 1960s when there was a proposal to develop a high-grade east–west track across the Kawekas. Considering the rather precipitous nature of the Mohaka Valley, the track is generally easy, although it does have a couple of high sidles above the river to avoid bluffs. About 40 minutes from the hut, the river takes a striking S–bend, with an impressive cliff on the far bank. The track zigzags steeply onto a shoulder with a view of a straight section of the river, here featuring an island. There is much more mature beech forest now, particularly on the true left. From here to the hut the track remains fairly level.

Although it has bunk space for 24, Te Puia Lodge is popular with school groups, hunters and anglers so can get quite full on weekends. If you're after seclusion, it's probably best to take a tent and camp at the Mangatainoka Hot Springs; and when deer hunters infiltrate the valley during the Roar (late March and early April) it's best to avoid the area altogether. The lodge lies on an open flat beside a beach and rapid in the Mohaka. After settling into the hut and enjoying a cup of tea, most visitors choose to wander up-river to the Mangatainoka Hot Springs for an evening soak. After crossing the Makino River on a swingbridge, the track sidles around the Mohaka to a steepish clamber up a narrow spur. This leads onto a flat terrace and finally down to the river flats again. Here, surrounding a good camping area, are some fine podocarps – including rimu, matai and kahikatea – with the hot springs nearby. Surrounded by a deck are two fibreglass tubs, which are filled with an adjustable pipe fed by hot water issuing from a bank. If the pools are cold on arrival, you may need to wait 30 minutes or so before the water reaches a suitably languorous temperature. The upper tub overflows into the lower one, and some scoops provide a means of adjusting the temperature in each. Taking a soak is a great way to relax during the evening, perhaps sipping some wine as you listen to the moreporks or even – if you're lucky – a North Island brown kiwi.

If the moon is not out, you'll need torches for the stroll back to Te Puia Lodge. The following day, it's simply a matter of walking back out. Alternatively, if you prefer a longer round trip, you can climb up to Makino Hut and walk the Makino Track back out to Makahu Road. Either way, back at the carpark you may as well have one last soak in the Mangatutu Hot Springs.

Trampers in Mangatainoka hot pools

Ascent of Kaweka J

Duration 1–2 days

Grade Medium

Times Makahu Saddle to Dominie Biv (2 bunks): 1.5–2 hours. Dominie to Kaweka J: 1–1.5 hours. Kaweka J to Back Ridge Hut (4 bunks, wood-stove, $5/night): 2–3 hours.

Maps U20 Kaweka, Kaweka Forest Parkmap

Access From Napier drive 60 km to Puketitiri. The tarseal ends 4 km past Puketitiri. Here turn left onto Whittle Road, follow it for 4 km, then turn right onto Kaweka Road. Follow this for 8 km, up a steep section, past Littles Clearing to the Makahu Saddle carpark, where there is a toilet, picnic table and information panel. Chains may be necessary in winter. Allow 90 minutes to drive from Napier.

Alternative Routes Those who prefer a day trip can simply climb to Kaweka J and return. Those wanting a slightly longer overnight trip can go on to climb North Kaweka from Back Ridge Hut, then descend eastwards on Pinnacle Spur to intercept the Kaweka Flats Track, which is followed back to Makahu Saddle. This involves some steep off-track tramping down Pinnacle Spur.

Information DOC Hawke's Bay Area Office, Ph 06 834 3111

Kaweka J is the highest peak in the Kaweka Range at 1724 metres, and the fourth-highest non-volcanic peak in the North Island after Hikurangi, Mangaweka (both in the Ruahine Range) and Makorako (in the Kaimanawa Range). It's an accessible and popular summit that is reached from Makahu Saddle, a high plateau lying to the east, and as the start point lies at the lofty altitude of 970 metres, the ascent is not as demanding as for those peaks mentioned above. From the top there are views across the North Island stretching from the Pacific Ocean and Hawke Bay in the east, to the volcanic plateau in the west. There's a biv en route and a hut at the end of the day.

From Makahu Saddle, the Kaweka Range rises abruptly in front of you, several semi-forested spurs joining the ridge crest like ribs to a backbone. This severely eroded part of the range has suffered heavily under human influence, with a chequered history of fires, sheep grazing, damage by deer and disastrous revegetation programmes that used lodgepole pine (*Pinus contorta*), which unfortunately later proved to be an aggressive weed. Under the glaring and revealing light of a summer sun the area does not have an attractive outlook by any means, but under a mantle of winter snow it can assume the appearance of a softer and more likeable landscape.

Despite its scenic shortcomings, the 750-metre climb to Kaweka J is not without reward. From the carpark, a signposted track leads past Makahu Saddle Hut (4 bunks, open fire, $5/night) then begins a zigzag ascent of Trials Spur. During summer there is scant water on these tops, and you'll need to carry plenty with you. The track used to push through lodgepole pine, but in a concerted effort DOC has recently felled all those in the area. You soon reach the subalpine herbfields, where Trials Spur joins the upper Makahu Spur. Ten minutes from here is Dominie Biv, perched on a flat shoulder with commanding views of North Kaweka. There's a water tank at the biv, which makes it a convenient spot to have some lunch or peruse the hut book.

Above the biv, the climb continues along a well-travelled route that is both poled and clearly defined. It sidles around a few rocky outcrops, then the gradient begins to ease off near the crest of the range. On top, you intercept a poled route. Head south, where a flat section of tops leads ever so slightly upwards to Kaweka J. Apart from a battered trig and a large cairn here (originally built by the Heretaunga Tramping Club as a memorial to members lost in World War II, and added to by generations of trampers ever since), you could be forgiven for not knowing this is the summit of the Kawekas, so undulating is the terrain. There are extensive views in every direction, with the rumpled, forested ridges of the Kawekas and Kaimanawas finally giving way to the more desolate terrain of the central volcanoes on the western horizon.

The Kawekas receive less rainfall than areas further west or north, and at first the tops here appear a little barren. But closer inspection reveals quite a diversity of alpine plants,

Dawn over Makahu Spur, Kaweka Forest Park

ranging from bluebells to the prostrate and curved-leaf *Dracophyllum recurvum*, two species of mountain daisy, rock cushion, a speargrass, a bristly carrot and the buttercup korikori. These plants mostly grow in the slight shelter provided by small scree hummocks, where they can partly escape the desiccating wind. In winter, the Kaweka Range can get heavy dumps of snow, particularly from easterly storms, and the plants have different pressures to cope with. Trampers, too, should note that the tops can be treacherous in bad weather, as they are exposed to winds from every direction.

Back Ridge Hut

After adding a couple of rocks to the cairn, head off down towards a poled route that leads to Back Ridge Hut. In misty conditions you'll need to pay sharp attention to your map, and compass work may be essential to find the correct spur. There are two spurs that lead westward to Back Ridge Hut: one that branches off very near Kaweka J and another that does so about a kilometre to the north. Take the more southerly spur, which descends gently and gets better defined as you go. Once you reach the bush edge, it's a short distance to Sterns Saddle, where a track branches off steeply to Back Ridge Hut. This lies in an attractive hollow beside a patch of mountain beech forest with a babbling brook nearby.

Back Ridge Hut is one of only two surviving deer culler huts constructed using Dexion aluminium framing (the other being Makahu Saddle Hut). The New Zealand Forest Service built it in 1957 with materials air-dropped from a plane. Later huts could be built using timber frames, as by then helicopters enabled these more bulky materials to be transported into the back country. The hut is painted a traditional Forest Service orange, and along with its surrounds, it seems to embody the Kaweka experience. So many of the huts in the park – including Tira Lodge, Ballard, Studholme Saddle, Kiwi Saddle, Mangaturutu, Manson and Back Ridge Biv – occupy sites just on the bush edge, often in small, attractive clearings whose edges are lapped by subalpine plants. It's a subtle sort of beauty, lacking the sharp peaks of the Ruahines or the bold summits of the Tararuas, but with appeal nonetheless.

The following day, follow the track that climbs steeply onto a spur to the north of the hut, then ascend at a more leisurely pace to the crest of the Kaweka Range. This spur is liberally poled, and you shouldn't have any navigation problems as long as you keep going uphill. Once back on the poled route leading across the main range, it seems a shame not to make an excursion to North Kaweka (1707 m) now you're so close. This is a rocky eminence with more form than its slightly higher neighbour, Kaweka J. Ambitious parties may scramble down the aptly named Pinnacle Spur to intercept the Kaweka Flats Track, but most simply retrace their footsteps back down Makahu Spur.

Kiwi Saddle

Duration 2–3 days

Grade Medium–Hard

Times Cameron carpark to Kiwi Saddle Hut (8 bunks, woodstove, $5/night): 3.5–4 hours. Kiwi Saddle to Kiwi Mouth Hut (4 bunks, open fire, $5/night) via Kiwi Creek: 2.5–3 hours; via track: 3 hours. Kiwi Mouth Hut to Cameron Hut (6 bunks, open fire, $5/night): 2.5–3 hours. Cameron Hut to road: 3– 4 hours.

Maps U20 Kaweka, Kaweka Forest Park Map

Access From Napier or Taihape, drive to Kuripapango on the Napier–Taihape Road. About 3 km east of Kuripapango is the Cameron carpark and picnic area and the start of the track to Kiwi Saddle Hut.

Alternative Route It's possible to shorten the trip by dropping down to Cameron Hut along a track that branches off near Kiwi Saddle Hut.

Information DOC Hawke's Bay Area Office, Ph 06 834 3111

This interesting weekend tramp in the southern part of Kaweka Forest Park offers a variety of terrain, with some ridge travel, good views and a day in the mighty Ngaruroro River. Those with angling inclinations may like to carry a portable rod as the Ngaruroro River is one of the best fly-fishing rivers in the North Island, renowned for its large rainbow trout. However, beware of tramping the turbulent Ngaruroro when in flood; it is not a river to be taken lightly. The route described here links three huts, completing a tidy circuit that begins and ends near Kuripapango on the Napier–Taihape Road.

Kuripapango, like other inland Hawke's Bay settlements, is now a mere shadow of its former self. In the late 19th and early 20th centuries it was an important staging post on the road connecting Hawke's Bay with Taihape. For a brief period, it was also a fashionable recreation retreat for Hawke's Bay folk, when it had two sizeable hotels. Completion of the main trunk line in 1905 dramatically reduced traffic through the area, and the road to Kuripapango remains winding and metalled even today.

From the Cameron carpark, a track leads down to the Ngaruroro River, where you cross the Waikarekare Stream on a footbridge. From here, a track begins a steep 750-metre climb through manuka and koromiko forest and beyond to Kuripapango.

The forests here are largely regenerating after a long history of fires and grazing, which for a while left the area largely bereft of any vegetation. In 1848, missionary-explorer William Colenso commented that the country was of the 'utmost desolate description'. These days, once you emerge above the bushline, views of the landscape still reveal significant scars, but it's not without beauty. The regeneration of native forest is encouraging, even if parts of it are threatened by the spread of lodgepole pine. Bluebells, foxgloves, eyebrights and *Dracophyllum recurvum* prove attractive here when in flower, and can be enjoyed as the track takes on a slightly easier gradient.

The track sidles just below Kuripapango (1250 m) and onto the ridge to the northwest. Good views unfold of the eroded Kaweka Range to the north, the tip of the Ruahine Range to the south and the more distant peaks of the volcanic interior. Far below, the Ngaruroro snakes in graceful curves, sometimes almost doubling back on itself.

A gradual climb to Pt 1359 ensues, from where the undulating track leads past a turn-off to Cameron Hut and finally onto a scree descent to Kiwi Saddle. Sitting in a patch of mountain beech on the bush edge is the tidy eight-bunk Kiwi Saddle Hut. The original hut was constructed here in 1947 by the Hastings-based Heretaunga Tramping

Misty dawn over Ngaruroro River, near Kiwi Mouth

Club, which also built the current one in 1987. Beyond the hut, marked tracks lead across a mixture of beech and manuka to a junction where there's a choice of two routes to Kiwi Mouth Hut: the wet-weather track over Pt 1238 or the route down Kiwi Creek. Unless the weather dictates otherwise, the latter is by far the best option as it's both quicker and easier.

A short track drops sharply to Kiwi Creek, which winds between steep banks covered in mountain beech. Although numerous crossings are required, travel down to the confluence with the Ngaruroro River is straightforward, and you may see New Zealand falcon en route. At the confluence lies the four-bunk Kiwi Mouth Hut, used by a mixture of anglers, hunters, trampers and the occasional rafting party. It's a good place to spend the night.

From the hut, a track leads downstream on the true left of the Ngaruroro River, past a swingbridge that crosses to the Manson Hut track, and beyond for about a kilometre until it ends, depositing you in the river bed. The Ngaruroro River is of a considerable size here, having drained most of the western catchments of Kaweka Forest Park and some of the southeastern Kaimanawa Range too. It has numerous rapids, some large, deep pools and a few sections of sizeable boulders. Travel downriver is only possible in good weather, and even then you will need to be familiar with river-crossing techniques. Tramping the Ngaruroro involves making numerous crossings, hopping over shingle beds beside the river and elbowing through forested shortcuts between river bends.

Tramper admires beech forest near Kuripapango, Kaweka Forest Park

About halfway down, it's possible to use a track that sidles along the true right bank to avoid a section of large rapids, then crosses a swingbridge to the true left. At times of normal river flow, however, this section is negotiable without using the track. A short distance downstream lies Cameron Hut, which makes a convenient lunch stop. Still remaining are a few hours of river travel, but on a sunny summer's day this presents no chore – there are plenty of places for swimming and on occasions you may see blue duck. The first sign that you're near the end is a particularly sharp U-bend in the river. A short distance downstream is a cableway and water gauge, from where it's just a 15-minute walk back to the carpark.

Zekes Hut

HIHITAHI FOREST SANCTUARY

Duration 2 days

Grade Easy–Medium

Times SH 1 to Hihitahi Trig:
1.5–2 hours. Trig to Zekes Hut:
40–60 minutes.

Map T21 Taihape

Access Access to Zekes Hut
begins from a paddock off SH
1, 10 km south of Waiouru and
20 km north of Taihape. A DOC
signpost at a farm gate marks
the entrance.

Information DOC Palmerston
North, 06 350 9700

The Central North Island contains landscapes not replicated elsewhere in New Zealand; undulating red tussock grasslands, set against a backdrop of the volcanoes of Tongariro National Park. There's a South Island flavour in the tussock grasslands, but the unmistakable presence of the volcanoes leaves no doubt about which island you are in.

Another less appreciated feature of this part of the country are pahautea – or mountain cedar (*Libocedrus bidwillii*) – forests. These once covered a vast area of some 300 square kilometres from near Waiouru to the northern Ruahine Range, forming dark, conical canopies over large tracts of hill and mountain country. Fires (predominantly lit by pre-European Maori but also Pakeha farmers) and, more recently, possums have sadly reduced these forests to fragments of their former range and splendour. However the Hihitahi Forest Sanctuary near Waiouru represents an accessible remnant, now with the added attraction of a new hut.

In 2007 DOC replaced an aged hunters' hut called Zekes – the only public one in the sanctuary – with a cosy four-bunker, part of a recent hut-building boom that has seen a whole crop of new huts grace the back country. A good track leads into the hut, offering trampers an excellent overnight trip.

After parking your car on the grassy paddock out of sight of SH 1, climb over a fence stile and follow a fenceline down a sloping paddock to a willow-lined stream. Sporadic marker poles indicate the route. Cross the swingbridge over the stream, follow the fenceline across a boggy, cattle-pugged paddock (which could be very muddy during a wet winter) and climb a grassy slope leading to the edge of the sanctuary. A large red pole marks the stile over a fence where the track enters the bush. Allow a total of about 25–30 minutes to reach the bush edge from SH 1.

After initially sidling, the track crosses a small stream and begins a brief but steep climb until gaining the ridge proper. Here, travel becomes undulating with a much more gradual incline. Totara – with occasional rimu and miro – dominates the canopy at first, while the understorey has maire, horopito, kamahi and wineberry. Higher up pahautea begins to make a presence, becoming more dominant the higher you climb. During summer long-tailed cuckoos add their noisy calls to those of other forest birds.

The forest opens out onto a small clearing at Hihitahi (1116 m), its summit trig now reduced to just wooden piles. Extensive mountain cedar forests surround the summit, and more are visible on the Mangaohane Plateau in the distant Ruahine Range. There's a fine view of Mt Ruapehu, barely 20 km away, and Mt Ngauruhoe too.

From the summit, the track – marked with orange triangles – descends to the north briefly before arcing around to the east amongst some very fine stands of pahautea. Their bark often peels off in strips to reveal reddish-brown wood.

Eventually the track leaves the ridge abruptly, and descends over an old grassy slip for some distance before re-entering the forest and sidling along forested slopes in the

Zekes Hut, Hihitahi Forest Sanctuary

Kaitapo Stream headwaters. Zekes Hut is located near a prominent fork in the stream, overlooking the surrounding forest. Sadly, possums have ravaged many of the nearby pahautea trees, which form stark pale skeletons amongst the greenery.

The superb little hut has four bunks, a good woodstove, a small deck, a water tank and much charm. Like many of the new DOC huts, Zekes has well-insulated walls to help keep in the warmth during winter.

While there aren't any options for making a round trip, the return journey over your inward route is short and pleasant enough for that not to matter.

Pahautea trees, Hihitahi Forest Sanctuary

Iron Gates, Triangle & Rangiwahia

Duration 2–3 days

Grade Medium

Times Table Flat Road to Alice Nash Memorial Heritage Lodge (8 bunks, woodstove, $5/night): 45 minutes. Alice Nash Memorial Heritage Lodge to Iron Gates Hut (7 bunks, woodstove, $5/night): 3–4 hours. Iron Gates Hut to Triangle Hut (6 bunks, woodstove, $5/night): 2.5–3 hours. Triangle Hut to Rangiwahia Hut (12 bunks, gas heater and cooking rings, $15/night): 4–5 hours. Rangiwahia Hut to Renfrew Road: 2 hours.

Maps T22 Mangaweka, U22 Ongaonga, Ruahine Forest Parkmap

Access From the Manawatu town of Feilding, drive 28 km to Kimbolton on SH 54. Just north of here, turn onto Apiti Road, which soon becomes Oroua Valley Road. After about 12 km Table Flat Road branches off on the right. The tramp ends at Renfrew Road, where there is a carpark and toilet.

Alternative Routes Both Rangiwahia and Iron Gates huts make good weekend destinations for those wanting a shorter trip without the need for juggling transport.

Information DOC Palmerston North Area Office, Ph 06 350 9700

This is a classic Ruahine weekend trip with a mixture of tramping terrain, attractive rivers that offer good swimming, four huts, tussock tops, interesting forests and fine views of the volcanic plateau. Completing the round trip will require a bit of car juggling; alternatively, you could just walk one way to Triangle Hut from either end.

The track starts from Table Flat Road, where there's a carpark with views of Mts Ruapehu and Ngauruhoe, and – on a clear day – even Mt Taranaki. A well-benched track sidles across farmland, down to Umutoi Creek, where an attractive arched bridge leads into Ruahine Forest Park. From here, a gradual climb ensues on what was once an old logging road to a track junction. The left fork leads down to the Oroua River flats and the route upstream, while the right-hand branch heads towards the Alice Nash Memorial Heritage Lodge and the wet-weather track.

The Oroua River flats provide good camping spots, and travel up-valley from here follows the Oroua River itself. This is not a route for those who aren't confident about river travel and should only be tackled when the water level is low. On a hot summer's day, however, this is great tramping, punctuated by an occasional dip in one of the many pools upstream.

The alternative wet-weather track takes about the same time and follows a well-benched track up-valley, often sidling quite high above the river. A few minutes past the track junction on the wet-weather track lies the new Alice Nash Memorial Heritage Lodge. The hut was built in 2007 by the Manawatu branch of the New Zealand Deerstalkers Association through a donation by the Nash family, replacing the old 18-bunk Heritage Lodge, which burnt down in 2005. The new hut makes a good destination in itself for anyone wanting a very short trip, or as an introduction to tramping for young children.

The western side of the Ruahine Range is botanically more diverse than the east, where fairly uniform beech forests dominate. In the west, higher rainfall supports varied podocarp–hardwood forests, including some attractive groves of pahautea (mountain cedar). Rimu, miro, kamahi and mahoe are just some of the trees encountered along the wet-weather track – luckily, the loggers did not penetrate any further up-valley.

The track dips to cross a few substantial tributaries of the Oroua, of which Tunupo Creek is the most boisterous (as there's no bridge here, it could present a problem when in flood). Iron Gates Hut lies on a grassy terrace above the Oroua River, reached after three or four hours from the Alice Nash Memorial Heritage Lodge.

Upstream of Iron Gates Hut, the tramping becomes more difficult. Triangle Hut lies past a formidable gorge in the Oroua River and can only be reached in reasonable weather and with low water levels. The reward for travel here is the chance to encounter blue ducks, and a growing sense that you are deep in the heart of the Ruahine mountains. At first there's a few boulder-strewn river crossings, past an island in the river, then a sharp 300-metre climb over a prominent spur to avoid the most tortuous section of the gorge. The start of this track is marked by a large orange triangle on the true right of a tributary (not the true left, as marked on the topographical map).

Trampers on Whanahuia Range

Upstream, the route meanders back and forth across the river, requiring numerous crossings. In places, the forest overhangs, lending the stream an almost sylvan feel. Higher up, near Triangle Hut, large floods have swept the banks clear of live vegetation and strewn logs about, testimony to both the power of rivers in high flow and the large catchment of the Oroua.

Triangle Hut sits back from the river, also on a grassy terrace and near a prominent river fork. If this is your first day, you'll probably want to stop here for the night, but those taking a more leisurely three days may want to contemplate camping on the tops of the Whanahuia Range. Opposite

Triangle Hut, a track ascends steeply through beech forest, which merges into pahautea and leatherwood near the bushline. Once through the subalpine scrub, you finally emerge onto tussock.

Poles lead towards Pt 1635 but then sidle off to a broad, flat saddle where there are reasonable campsites and some nearby tarns for water. On a calm, fine evening this is a great spot to contemplate very little other than the changes in the colour of the sky over the nearby ranges.

From the tarns, the track climbs steadily up a well-defined path onto a knob just before Mangahuia (1583 m). From here, there are broad views of the Ruahine Range, stretching from Te Hekenga down to Tunupo, as well as the more distant peaks of the volcanic plateau.

Past a signpost, a gentle 3-kilometre stroll leads down the well-poled tussock ridge towards the bushline, and Rangiwahia Hut. The original hut – an old shepherds' shelter constructed in 1930 – was expanded by the newly formed Rangiwahia Ski Club in 1938. The club winched a bulldozer up a spur to level some slopes, and installed a rope tow that was powered by an Indian motorbike. Skiing was popular here for a brief period, and the club peaked at 80 members, but disbanded after World War II. In 1967 the New Zealand Forest Service rebuilt the deteriorating hut, and offered it to the newly-formed Palmerston North Tramping and Mountaineering Club. Club members managed to maintain the hut over the next 16 years, but by 1983 lacked the resources to fund a badly-needed new hut. So during 1983–84 the Forest Service once again stepped in, and – with volunteer assistance – demolished the previous hut and constructed the present (fourth) Rangiwahia Hut.

Whanahuia Range at dawn

Despite suitable topography, in these days of warmer winters and poorer snowfall the area has limited ski potential, but a really good dump does entice the occasional ski tourer.

From Rangiwahia Hut you are once again on a well-graded track, which soon descends through subalpine scrub and pahautea forest to another attractive arched bridge, this one spanning an impressively narrow chasm some 70 metres deep. Beyond, the track sidles out to Renfrew Road and is easy going apart from a detour where the original track has slipped away. The rough and rooty detour track climbs above the slip, taking 35–40 minutes, and rejoins the benched track about 30 minutes from the Renfrew Road carpark.

Sawtooth Ridge

Duration 2–3 days

Grade Hard

Times Mill Road to Daphne Hut (12 bunks, woodstove, $5/night) via Tukituki River: 2.5–3 hours. Daphne Hut to Howletts Hut (8 bunks, woodstove, $5/night): 2 hours. Howletts Hut to Tarn Biv (2 bunks) via Sawtooth Ridge: 5–6 hours. Tarn Biv to Tukituki River and roadend via Rosvalls Track: 3–4 hours.

Map U22 Ongaonga

Access From SH50, some 10 km south of Ongaonga, turn onto Makaretu Road. After 4 km turn left onto Mill Road and follow this until you halt at a locked gate on a farm, near a woolshed. The legal access to the Tukituki River begins about 200 m further along this road, where a DOC and Fish & Game sign indicates the start of the track.

Alternative Route It's also possible to reach Daphne Hut from a track that starts from Kashmir Road.

Information DOC Hawke's Bay Area Office, Ph 06 834 3111

From some profiles the Sawtooth Ridge looks as formidable a prospect as its name suggests, but in reality this section of the Ruahine Range is not that steep, and in everything but windy or winter conditions it is well within the abilities of most experienced trampers. The tramp begins from the Tukituki River, climbs to Howletts Hut and then traverses the Sawtooth to Tarn Biv, from where it descends back to the river. For those not wishing to tackle the ridge itself, all three huts on this round trip make worthwhile destinations in their own right.

From the DOC sign at the end of Mill Road, follow a poled route down an old road to the Tukituki River, which ends about 10 minutes downstream of the confluence with Moorcock Stream. To start with, the gravelly river is not particularly attractive, but it does provide fast travel upstream. After about 30 minutes, you reach a signposted junction marking the end of Rosvalls Track.

Upstream, the Tukituki becomes more boulder-strewn, and beech forest begins to crowd in over the banks. After a further two hours, past an attractive stand of rimu trees, you reach another signposted junction where a track leads off to Kashmir Road (an alternative entry point). Just upriver, the Tukituki enters a small gorge that can be difficult to pass in times of flood. Once through the gorge, the river opens to a stream junction where three prominent spurs meet. You'll climb one of these to reach Howletts Hut, but first it's worth taking a break at nearby Daphne Hut. The hut lies on a small flat about 100 metres upstream on the Tukituki's true left. It has an unusual A-frame design and was built in 1986 by the Takapau Lions Club.

Sawtooth Ridge

The track up Daphne Spur starts steeply, like most of those in the V-shaped river valleys of the North Island mountain axis. After climbing for 200 metres, it eases off a little and the spur begins to narrow as you tramp steadily upwards. In places, the track is quite eroded, and there are some big steps for those with short legs! After a brief section through subalpine scrub, the track gains Daphne Ridge, where Howletts Hut lies in a sheltered hollow overlooking the north branch of the Tukituki.

This is a grand spot with commanding views, and it comes as no surprise to learn that a number of different huts have occupied the site. A Hawke's Bay schoolteacher and botanist, William Howlett, built the original hut in 1893 out of split mountain cedar. It lasted until about 1930, then in 1938 construction of a replacement hut was begun by the then Ruahine Tramping Club (Palmerston North) and the Heretaunga Tramping Club (Hawke's Bay). This hut was opened in 1940. The current hut was built by the latter club in 1978–79, with minor improvements since. Like Daphne, Howletts has an unusual design, but it is very comfortable – especially on a winter's night with the potbelly stove glowing.

The Sawtooth Ridge can't be seen clearly from Howletts Hut – it first comes into view about an hour along Daphne Ridge. After leaving the hut, a rough track passes through a brief section of stunted forest then sidles around scree and tussock slopes (there's a tarn for water near here). A steady climb up tussock slopes ensues, leading onto a knoll beneath Tiraha. From here, the Sawtooth does indeed look impressive, its broken spine dropping sharply into very steep, eroded gullies. During winters past, when cold weather was more reliable, climbers used to practise their ice-climbing skills in these gullies.

As the direct approach to Tiraha is very steep, most trampers opt to reach it by first

Sunrise at Howletts Hut

sidling onto a small tussock spur that branches off to the southeast. From Tiraha (1668 m), marked by a large cairn, the Sawtooth Ridge lies spread out before you, no longer looking much like a saw, or at most a very blunt one. Although steep-sided, the actual ridge crest is quite rounded, and any narrow sections are easily negotiated by well-defined sidles. Still, in windy conditions it can prove nerve-wracking, and a traverse in winter requires sound mountaineering skills.

The steepest sections all come in the first 1.5 kilometres, and most can be passed by sidling to the east. Where the ridge is narrower, the track is quite well defined and intermittent cairns mark the way. On the flatter sections beyond, you begin a climb up to Ohuinga (1686 m). Note that first you reach a bump that might be mistaken for Ohuinga – the real one is further north. From Ohuinga, three ridges branch off, and in misty conditions getting the right one onto Black Ridge (which heads southeast) may require taking a compass bearing. A steep drop leads to a saddle, followed by a climb around a couple of knolls that finally leads onto undulating, tarn-studded slopes. These make the ideal spot for an extended lunch break. Black Ridge provides views of perhaps the most impressive profile of the Sawtooth, and now you can relax in the knowledge that the hard part is over.

At the end of Black Ridge is the recently renovated Tarn Biv, a tidy two-bunk dog-box with an open-air longdrop. From here, a well-marked track leads through gnarled mountain beech forest to a rocky knoll (1285 m) where there is a signposted track junction. One track leads straight down to Daphne Hut, while the other, Rosvalls Track (the quickest route), drops directly to the Tukituki River further east. Once in the Tukituki Valley, simply retrace your previous day's route back to the farm and your vehicle.

McKinnon Hut & Kawhatau River

Duration 2–3 days

Grade Medium

Times Kawhatau Base to McKinnon Hut (6 bunks, wood-stove, $5/night): 4–5 hours. McKinnon Hut to Crow Hut (6 bunks, wood-stove, $5/night): 2 hours. Crow Hut to carpark via tops: 3.5–4 hours. Crow Hut to carpark via river: 5–6 hours.

Maps U22 Ongaonga, Ruahine Parkmap

Access At Mangaweka turn off SH 1 onto the Kawhatau Valley Road. Follow this for 20 km to Kawhatau, then take the Upper Kawhatau and Rangitane roads for 13 km to reach the Kawhatau Base Hut. Permission should be sought from the farmer to cross the last section of road through a patch of private bush.

Alternative Route From McKinnon Hut, trampers can traverse the Hikurangi Range over Mangaweka (the highest peak of the Ruahine Range) to Purity Hut (5–7 hours). For more information, see the Purity Hut chapter (page 147).

Information DOC Palmerston North Area Office, Ph 06 350 9700

McKinnon Hut occupies the northern end of the Hikurangi Range, overlooking the Kawhatau River and the Mokai Patea Range. It's a great destination for a weekend tramp, encompassing some bush, tops and river travel. And perhaps best of all, there's a choice of routes down the Kawhatau River to complete a satisfying round trip.

Park your car next to the Kawhatau Base Hut, which is an ex-Forest Service base now available for booking through DOC (10 bunks, wood-stove, showers, electric lighting, $10/night). The track to McKinnon Hut starts 100 metres back along the road, marked by a signpost, and descends down to a cableway over the Kawhatau River.

The former New Zealand Forest Service established these cableways across rivers where

133

McKinnon Hut and the Mokai Patea Range, Ruahine Forest Park

the span was considered too large for a conventional swingbridge. Essentially they consist of a cage (suitable for only one person) which whizzes down a wire cable spanning the width of the river. At the cable's lowest ebb your companions wind you over the remaining (uphill) span using winches located on either side. Riding the cage downhill is quite fun, providing you've kept your head and hair well clear of the winding mechanism.

Solo trampers can use an internal winder to winch themselves across, but should check the cage before getting in. There's a story of one tramper who discovered too late that the winder was missing, and remained suspended in the cage until another party of trampers happened upon him a couple of days later.

If river levels are low, it may be easier and quicker for a large party just to descend to the river and splash across. On the far side of the cableway, the track climbs onto the Hikurangi Range. It's one of the steepest in the Ruahine Range – which is really saying something. Fortunately the climb is not totally unrelenting, and a few flat spots allow you to regain your composure for the next push.

A steep climb is, however, a quick climb, and pahautea (mountain cedar) trees begin to appear amongst the mountain beech forest as you approach the bushline. Soon afterward, the track emerges onto the sprawling tussock grasslands of the Hikurangi Range. Here a well-poled route marks the way over the undulating tops, with increasingly good views of the Mokai Patea, an unusually flat-topped range on the far side of the Kawhatau

Valley. Good travel leads over the tops on the fairly well-worn track. Mats of white daisy and the distinctive *Dracophyllum recurvum* add botanical interest in places, and views of Mt Ruapehu unfold when the weather is clear.

An old lichen-encrusted signpost marks the track to Crow Hut. Carry on along the tops, passing a large tarn, which makes a good spot for lunch. A further climb leads to Pt 1625, where McKinnon Hut can be seen below, perched on a ledge above the bushline. A steep descent down a sometimes-muddy track reaches the hut.

The tidy 6-bunk, ex-Forest Service hut typifies the good work completed in Ruahine Forest Park by DOC in recent years. Without changing the overall size or character of the hut, they have added a new wood burner, given the hut a fresh lick of paint, replaced the mattresses, and installed a map with route information.

The hut's commanding location provides a good vantage point from which to study the map and work out the surrounding terrain. Clearly visible are Waipawa Saddle and Te Atuaoparapara on the main Ruahine Range, the headwaters of the Kawhatau River, and even a track leading up onto the Mokai Patea Range.

From McKinnon Hut a track leads down to the middle reaches of the Kawhatau River, and a short distance downstream, Crow Hut. Below McKinnon, the track starts off reasonably gently, passing through some large broadleaf trees – at a height just out of reach of browsing deer – which sadly have no seedlings beneath them. The spur soon steepens, offering knee-jarring travel amongst gnarled tree roots, until you reach the river. Here the Kawhatau flows tightly between steep banks, with impressive mountain cabbage trees standing like sentinels on either side.

Kawhatau River near the McKinnon Hut Track, Ruahine Forest Park

Bouldery travel downriver ensues; the sort of terrain that is impossible and dangerous when the river is in flood. Crow Hut, another tidy 6-bunker, is about 30 minutes downstream.

According to information inside, the hut owes its name to the kokako. Kokako, once commonly called blue-wattled crows, were apparently last observed in the Ruahines around the Crow Hut vicinity as late as the 1940s.

From Crow Hut there are two options for finishing a weekend-length tramp. The first is a rather slow but exciting scramble down the gorges of the lower Kawhatau River back to the roadend. This is definitely only a trip for summer, when river levels are at their lowest and warmest. As there are a few places where you might have to swim, take dry bags and wear plenty of warm thermals.

The second option is to once again access the Hikurangi Range using a sharpish track that leads onto the tops up a spur directly behind Crow Hut. Like the other tracks in the area, this one makes no concessions to labouring lungs or crying calf muscles. At the bushline there are disturbing signs of a canopy collapse – no understorey save for thick *Gahnia* grass, with the trees widely spaced. Perhaps a combination of altitudinal stress and deer browsing offers no chance for seedling recruitment.

Once at the Crow Hut signpost that you passed the day before, it's simply a matter of heading out on your inward route.

Sunset on the Mokai Patea Range

Sunrise Hut & Waipawa Saddle

Duration 2 days

Grade Medium

Times North Block Road to Waipawa Forks Hut (12 bunks, woodstove, $5/night): 1 hour. Waipawa Forks Hut to Waipawa Saddle: 2 hours. Waipawa Saddle to Sunrise Hut (20 bunks, gas heater and cooking rings, $15/night): 3–4 hours. Sunrise Hut to Triplex Hut (12 bunks, woodstove, $5/night): 2–2.5 hours. Triplex Hut to roadend via Swamp Track: 30 minutes.

Map U22 Ongaonga

Access From SH50 just north of Ongaonga, turn left onto Wakarara Road. Follow this to Wakarara, where you turn left onto North Block Road. The road passes through several farm gates (keep them open or closed as you find them) before reaching the grassy carpark located a short distance from the Waipawa River.

Information DOC Hawke's Bay Area Office, Ph 06 834 3111

Sunrise Hut occupies one of the best tops locations in the Ruahine Range, and as it is serviced by a high-quality track, it has unsurprisingly become the park's most popular hut. While the hut is a fine destination in its own right, especially for families, those wanting a more challenging round trip can reach it via the Waipawa River and Te Atuaoparapara.

From the carpark on North Block Road, follow an old vehicle track down to the Waipawa River. Between floods, the lower Waipawa River is regularly choked with introduced lupin, which, while attractive in flower, can otherwise detract from the start of the tramp. However, travel proves easy on the shingly riverbed, and progress is swift up into the wilder reaches of the valley.

There's one small, narrow section of the river, too feeble to call a gorge, but a possible obstacle if the river is in flood. The 12-bunk Waipawa Forks Hut (situated on a ledge not visible from the riverbed) is reached on a 10-minute side track leading up from a signpost on the true right of the river.

Shortly upstream from the hut, on the opposite side of the valley, is a track that leads up to join the Sunrise Hut track. If the weather proves unsuitable for tops travel, this would make a good alternative route to the one described here. Otherwise, carry on climbing gradually up the Waipawa River, with the distinctive scoop of the Waipawa Saddle visible on the skyline ahead. Further up, the river becomes boulder-strewn, and subalpine scrub begins to close in on the banks. Look for the start of the track on a spur here. This well-worn track ends the final push to Waipawa Saddle, climbing through a fairly dense band of leatherwood.

A cairn and two waratahs mark the saddle, and there are views westwards over to the Hikurangi Range and the Ruahine interior. A short side trip, worth doing in summer, involves tramping down the headwaters of the Waikamaka River, perhaps as far as Waikamaka Hut. Initially steep and poled, the route soon drops into the riverbed. During spring *Ranunculus insignis* buttercups grow in profusion right by the stream edge, making the valley quite delightful.

Back at Waipawa Saddle, a sharp climb ensues up scree and alpine tussock slopes, without anything much in the way of cairns. Higher up, views unfold east over Hawke's Bay and north to the mountains of Tongariro National Park. There's a flat shelf here, with ample tarns for drinking water and a few places for camping. The diversity of alpine plants warrants a closer look – there's North Island edelweiss, eyebrights, at least two sorts of *Celmisia* daisies and the attractive rust-coloured *Ranunculus recurvum*.

Te Atuaoparapara has by now come into sharp profile, looking rather more precipitous than it actually is. To reach it, you initially drop down past some tarns to a small dip in the range, then begin a short but steep slog up scree slopes, keeping well to the west of the ridge crest. The final steepish pinch ends at a small trig station marking the top.

On a good day, the route to Sunrise Hut is clear: a big drop down to a scrubby saddle, then an undulating climb over a knob to Armstrong Saddle and the final stretch to Buttercup Hollow. The first part of the descent from Te Atuaoparapara follows a leading

Waikamaka River

138

spur down tussock slopes, to where a partially-defined route pushes through the scrub. Travel is sometimes a matter of finding tussock leads through patches of leatherwood. On the far side, where the ridge becomes defined again, a quite pronounced route leads up to a signposted knoll. Here, a side route branches off to Top Maropea Hut, which makes a quieter alternative to staying at Sunrise Hut. Continue past the junction down to Armstrong Saddle.

On the saddle, an interpretation panel describes the area's history. Back in July 1935, pioneer aviator Hamish Armstrong disappeared while on a flight from Dannevirke to Hastings. Some two weeks into an intensive search his wrecked Gypsy Moth was found crashed on the saddle. However, no trace of Armstrong was found, except for a shirt marked

Trampers in mist on Te Atuaoparapara, Ruahine Forest Park

'XXX'. Presumably, he survived the crash sufficiently uninjured to try to walk out but never made it.

A short stroll along a track that skirts some of the most impressive erosion scars in the park leads to the large and popular Sunrise Hut. It's perched in the sheltered Buttercup Hollow with commanding views eastwards, and there are a couple of formed campsites nearby. Originally an eight-bunk, Lockwood-style structure built by the former New Zealand Forest Service in the 1980s, the hut was enlarged significantly by DOC in 2005, increasing its capacity to 20 bunks.

From the hut, a well-benched track zigzags at a sedate gradient down a prominent spur. There are tree ferns aplenty, attractive red beech forest, some mountain cabbage trees and the occasional mistletoe protected by possum barriers. In recent years the track has been upgraded to make it ideal for family groups and less experienced trampers. About halfway down, the track to Waipawa Forks Hut branches off to the south.

Where the Sunrise Track reaches the flat terrain of the Swamp Track, another sign-posted side track branches off to Triplex Hut (where there is ample room for camping). Most trampers however bypass the hut and continue along the Swamp Track. Here, podocarp trees – including miro, kahikatea and rimu – intersperse with beech forest to give some sense of the lowland forests that once dominated much of Hawke's Bay. Listen out for kakariki and New Zealand falcon. After crossing a stile at the bush edge the track descends a short grassy slope back to the carpark.

Mid Pohangina Hut

RUAHINE FOREST PARK

Duration 2 days

Grade Medium

Times Tamaki West Road to Stanfield Hut (8 bunks, woodstove, $5/night) via river: 1.5 hours; via Holmes Ridge: 2 hours. Stanfield to Cattle Creek Hut (8 bunks, woodstove, $5/night): 2 hours. Cattle Creek to Mid Pohangina Hut (4 bunks, open fire, $5/night): 2–3 hours. Mid Pohangina to Pohangina Valley East Road: 4–6 hours.

Maps T23 Kimbolton, U23 Dannevirke, Ruahine Forest Parkmap

Access From SH 2 just south of Dannevirke, take Law Road to Ruaroa and then turn right onto Top Grass Road. Tamaki West Road branches off to the left of Top Grass Road, and after about 3 km there's a carpark next to a locked gate. The far end of the tramp is accessed on Pohangina Valley East Road, north of Ashhurst.

Alternative Route During periods of low flow it's possible to splash down the Pohangina River from Mid Pohangina Hut all the way out to farmland. This makes a great summer alternative, but it does take longer and requires negotiating some deep holes in gorged sections of the river.

Information DOC Palmerston North Area Office, Ph 06 350 9700

This tramp crosses the Ruahines at the lowest pass on the entire range, linking the Tamaki River on the east with Cattle Creek and the Pohangina River in the west. There are three huts and plenty of places for swimming, and it's probably the most painless way of completing a Ruahine crossing. It's also one of the few traverses possible in a weekend where the transport is not too difficult to organise.

From the Tamaki West Road carpark, go through a gate and walk for about 10 minutes to reach a grassy camping and picnic area, where there's a shelter, toilet and an information panel explaining the area's history. During the 1930s a mill operated here, hauling out large rimu by steam hauler, but it soon proved unprofitable. One of the bushmen, George Stanfield, later commented: 'The country was rough and difficult to work. No one made money and the foothills and basins would have been better left in virgin state.'

From the shelter, you can either tramp up the riverbed of the Tamaki River West Branch, or take the Holmes Ridge Track. Finding the start of the latter route involves crossing the river and pushing through buddleia to find a marked track that climbs briefly up to the Holmes Ridge Track. This is an old road put in by the New Zealand Forest Service for revegetation work during the 1970s, but is now largely grass-covered. Holmes Ridge offers good views of the valley, with rimu emergent over tree ferns.

However, if water levels are low the river is the best option. Past the shelter a track leads up-valley, (passing the signposted track to Travers Hut), before ending at a riverbank. From there it's an easy amble up-valley on the open, gravelly riverbed, crossing where necessary. In places introduced lupin and buddleia infest the banks, but floods regularly gouge them out. After about an hour or so, you pass a signpost at the end of the Holmes Ridge Track. Continue up-river for another 30 minutes to Stanfield Hut. This tidy hut (named after George Stanfield) has been improved in recent years, but you'll probably want to push on to Cattle Creek Hut anyway. A short distance upstream, a track begins a solid climb to a low, forested saddle on the Ruahine Range.

Tramper crosses swingbridge over Pohangina River

From the saddle, there are two possible routes to Cattle Creek Hut: via a track along a low section of the Ruahine Range, or down into the headwaters of Cattle Creek. While the latter is open and gravelly, the ridge route is probably more pleasant. It follows a track that leads through kamahi, totara and rata forest – along with some patches of leatherwood – for about 2 kilometres before reaching a junction where it leaves the main range and drops sharply down to Cattle Creek and the hut. This tidy hut lies on a terrace on the true left bank, just downstream of the point where the track emerges onto the river. Sadly, the devastation wrought by possums on the forest in this part of the Ruahines is all too evident, with many canopy trees dead or dying.

The next day, you follow Cattle Creek to its junction with the Pohangina River; this section is really the highlight of the trip, particularly on a warm summer's day. Initially, the river provides easy travel on gravel and boulders. After about an hour you reach a sizeable pool that you can either scramble around or swim through (which can be quite pleasant when it's hot). Further downstream, the creek enters a small but difficult gorge, where a waterfall halts progress. Getting past this obstacle involves negotiating a steep rocky bank on the true left using a chain installed by DOC.

After this rather exhilarating descent, another hour or so of river travel leads to a fairly large slip on the true right. It's possible to take a shortcut to Mid Pohangina Hut, crossing an obvious saddle near this slip. The hut is a very tidy four-bunker, set amongst some tall rimu trees. Alternatively, you can bypass the hut and continue down Cattle Creek to its junction with the Pohangina River.

Mid Pohangina Hut, Pohangina Valley

The Pohangina is a sizeable Ruahine river with a large catchment and is well-known for blue ducks. Several pairs occupy territories for most of the river's length, and recent research suggests that the Ruahines are one of the few places where numbers of this endangered waterfowl are actually increasing.

There's a swingbridge over the river about 300 metres upstream of the Cattle Creek confluence, leading onto the sidle track down-valley. The impressively green pools below the swingbridge are deep and ideal for swimming. It takes a full day to travel down through the gorges of the Pohangina River from Mid Pohangina Hut, with one pool to swim en route and another waterfall to negotiate below Centre Creek, and it's definitely a fine-weather trip only. However, in the right conditions the lower Pohangina provides classic river tramping.

The sidle track is really the only option in wet weather, and despite the ups and downs it provides much faster travel. From the swingbridge, the track climbs for a while before settling into some benched travel through mahoe, horopito and podocarp forest. Watch for ongaonga in the shadier sections. On occasions, there are good viewpoints over the river, revealing some of the valley's impressive slips.

Several small streams are crossed before the track reaches a junction where a side trail leads down to the site of the old Centre Creek Biv (now removed and no great loss) and a track that connects with Takapari Road. Continue along the main Pohangina Valley track, where the travel becomes easier as the valley opens out, eventually crossing Piripiri Stream on the edge of the farmland. Poles lead across river terraces, over the Te Ano Whiro Stream, then up a sharp farm track – fairly unwelcome at this end of the day – that climbs to the carpark at the Pakohu Scenic Reserve on Pohangina Valley East Road.

Ascent of Mangaweka

Mangaweka 1731m — Iron Peg 1703m — Wooden Peg 1672m — Maungamahue 1661m — alternate route to McKinnon Hut — HIKURANGI RANGE — WHANAHUIA RANGE — Purity Hut — Kelly Knight Hut — Hikurangi Strm — Pourangaki River — Pari Strm — carpark — Mangakukeke Rd to Upper Kawhatau, Mangaweka

Duration 2–3 days

Grade Medium

Times Mangakukeke Road to Purity Hut (6 bunks, woodstove, $5/night): 2.5–3 hours. Purity Hut to Wooden Peg: 1.5 hours. Wooden Peg to Mangaweka summit: 1 hour return. Wooden Peg to Kelly Knight Hut (8 bunks, woodstove, $5/night): 2–3 hours. Kelly Knight to road 2.5–3 hours.

Maps U22 Ongaonga, T22 Mangaweka, Ruahine Forest Parkmap

Access At Mangaweka turn off SH 1 onto the Kawhatau Valley Road. Follow this for 20 km to Kawhatau, then take the Upper Kawhatau Road for 3 km before turning off onto to Mangakukeke Road. Follow this for 3 km to the roadend, where there's a carpark, toilet and information panel. Although the route to Purity Hut is open all year round, access to Kelly Knight Hut requires permission from Bayfield Farm (Ph 06 382 5577), as the route crosses a section of private farmland. Access is usually restricted during calving (July to September).

Alternative Route With appropriate transport arrangements, from Purity Hut it's possible to traverse the Hikurangi Range past McKinnon Hut to Kawhatau Base (see page 137).

Information DOC Palmerston North Area Office, Ph 06 350 9700

Mangaweka (1731 m) is the highest point on the Ruahine Range, and is accessible from Purity Hut over a weekend trip. As well as two huts, some impressive rolling tussock tops and excellent views, this tramp also passes through some of the best stands of pahautea (mountain cedar) forest in the park. It's a good trip to make in northerly weather, as this inland part of the Ruahines often stays cloudy but dry when areas further north or west are wet. All in all, it is a satisfying round trip, especially for those who like peak-bagging.

From the carpark at Mangakukeke Road, a series of marker poles leads over muddy farmland, crossing one stream and then rising sharply beside a fenceline onto a spur. Once you are on the spur proper, you've reached the Ruahine Forest Park boundary and the gradient eases off somewhat for the rest of the climb up to Purity Hut. Red and silver beech dominate at first, with prickly

Purity Hut, Hikurangi Range, Ruahine Forest Park

shield fern on the forest floor. Higher up, the first of the pahautea trees makes an appearance, and 20 minutes later you're surrounded by a magnificent grove of them at the old Purity Hut site. No one will miss the rustic old three-bunker, as the new six-bunk Purity Hut occupies a much grander location just above the bushline, about 10 minutes further on. Built in 2006, Purity was the first new hut erected in the western Ruahine Range since the 1980s. It offers excellent views over the Rangitikei and Mt Ruapehu.

From Purity Hut a well-poled route pushes upwards through fairly lush tussock on a well-defined spur leading to the Hikurangi Range. By the time you reach Wooden Peg, most of the climbing is done. It is from here that trampers branch off the poled route for a side trip to Mangaweka. During inclement weather this section is certainly no place to lose your bearings. After dipping and climbing slightly to Iron Peg, undulating terrain leads to the rounded, unassuming summit of Mangaweka. A few bits of wood are all that remains of a battered trig station. Here, the views are panoramic, encapsulating the entire northern extent of the Ruahine Range as well as glimpses of distant Taranaki and Ruapehu.

From Wooden Peg, the poled route to the Pourangaki River continues, and as the spur is not well-defined these markers prove very welcome in misty conditions. During the descent to the bushline, tussock hides occasional speargrass that seemingly lies in wait to stab you. Near the bushline, there are some patches of leatherwood to push through and one steep scree slope to negotiate. In summer, tarns here provide water.

Once it enters the subalpine scrub, the track becomes well-marked, leading down into another stand of pahautea forest. The flaking, rust-coloured bark of these trees contrasts strongly with the mossy green undergrowth, providing an enchanting place for a rest. Further down the spur, mountain beech and the occasional totara eventually replace the

Hikurangi Range in winter

145

mountain cedar. The track descends at a fairly gentle gradient, before reaching a track junction marked by a cairn. Continue straight ahead down the spur if you don't want to visit Kelly Knight Hut, or turn sharp left if you do.

This latter section of track drops steeply down a bush face for 150 metres before intersecting the main Pourangaki Valley Track. Follow this up-valley a short distance, then cross a swingbridge over the Pourangaki River and walk a couple of hundred metres down the other side to a grassy flat where Kelly Knight Hut is situated. The tidy eight-bunk hut was built in 1975, upgraded in 1992, and is named after local hunter Kelly Knight.

The tramp out follows the well-graded and benched Pourangaki Valley Track, on the true right of the river. At one point there are good views of a narrow section of the river, but mostly you stroll through red beech forest that is punctuated by the occasional rimu. One-and-a-half hours from the hut, you emerge onto Bayfield Farm, where a flat 10-minute stroll over paddocks leads to a vehicle track. The Mangakukeke carpark is a further 30 minutes walk.

Tramper on the Hikurangi Range, with Mangaweka beyond

Northern Crossing

Duration 2–3 days

Grade Hard

Times Putara Road to Herepai Hut (10 bunks, wood-stove, $5/night): 2 hours. Herepai to Dundas Hut (6 bunks, $5/night): 5–7 hours. Dundas to Arete Biv (2 bunks): 3 hours. Arete to Te Matawai Hut (18 bunks, wood-stove, $5/night): 2.5 hours. Te Matawai to Waiopehu Hut (18 bunks, wood-stove, $5/night): 3 hours. Waiopehu to Poads Road: 4 hours.

Maps S25 Levin, Tararua Forest Parkmap

The Tararua Northern Crossing is a harder and less popular trip than its southern counterpart, but takes the keen tramper into a much less trammelled and wilder part of the range. Leslie Adkin, a Tararua enthusiast and founding member of the Levin–Waiopehu Tramping Club, was the first to complete a Northern Crossing in 1909. He and companion Bert Lancaster travelled up the Ohau River onto Dundas, crossed the Waiohine Pinnacles and Tarn Ridge, climbed Mitre and then descended along the Waingawa River. These days the most popular way to complete a Northern Crossing is still a traverse from the Ohau to the Waingawa, largely following Adkin's route. However, a more direct route (as described here) starts from the Putara Road end in the Wairarapa, traverses the lumpy Dundas Ridge and then exits down past the new Waiopehu Hut.

This is a demanding trip, and parties tackling the tramp over the course of a normal weekend will probably need to reach Herepai Hut on the Friday night. Alternatively, it makes a splendid three-day trip.

Access Turn off SH 2 at Eketahuna, following signs to Putara; these lead you onto Nireaha Road and Priests Road, and finally to Putara Road. The tramp ends across farmland to reach Poads Road (which is accessible off SH 57 at Levin on Tararua and Gladstone roads). Please respect this private land by sticking to the track, as future access depends on the goodwill of the farmers.

Alternative Routes From Te Matawai Hut it's possible to drop down to the Ohau River via the Yeates Track. This takes less time than the route described, but is a dry-weather route only (see Mangahao Flats, page 155). Waiopehu Hut makes a much shorter, though superb, destination for a weekend tramp.

Information DOC Kapiti Area Office, Ph 04 296 1112; DOC Wairarapa Area Office, Ph 06 377 0022

From the Putara Road end a signposted track leads into forest and soon crosses the Mangatainoka River on a swingbridge. Travel up-valley is along a gentle track, until another swingbridge is crossed, when a steepish ascent ensues to a bush-covered knoll. Here, a signposted track junction indicates the way to Herepai Hut (the other branch leads to Roaring Stag Lodge). Head right to Herepai, along a gentle downsloping ridge to a small dip. Herepai Hut is 10 minutes walk up the other side of the dip and is positioned on the bushline with imposing views of the circle of peaks ahead: Herepai, Ruapae and East Peak.

After a well-deserved break (or night) at the hut, continue following a track that ascends through subalpine scrub. The route becomes less defined as you climb, and the first real knob gained is Herepai. A small white cross (one of several encountered on the trip) lies just off the top and is inscribed with the name Stan Evans.

From here to Dundas Ridge, the track involves a considerable amount of up and down, with the trail barely defined in places. Indeed, it's very much a tactile experience, with the occasional gentle caress of leatherwood and travel through the tall tussocks conducted more by feel than sight. There are no poles and few cairns on the route, and in mist it can be a navigational challenge, especially in the reverse direction.

Nevertheless, on a clear day there are vistas of both the Manawatu and Wairarapa, and even the South Island and the distant peaks of Ruapehu and Taranaki can be visible. The next knob reached is Ruapae, which leads to a climb up East Peak. Here, the route turns sharply westwards, where a nasty, unwelcome 210-metre descent drops to a scrubby gap. This gap deserves the name of Hells Gate far more than that on the Southern Crossing, especially as a climb of almost the same height ensues up the other side to West Peak. The route changes direction abruptly once again on West Peak, striking southwest.

Late evening over Walker, West Peak and East Peak from Pukemoremore, Dundas Ridge

By this stage you're on Dundas Ridge, classic Tararua tops with some craggy peaks, few tarns and more than a little up and down travel. While it's fairly flat as far as Walker, Pukemoremore presents another climb, and by the time you reach the turn-off to Dundas Hut – marked by several cairns – you'll be feeling the effects of a big day's efforts. The tidy, six-bunk hut lies on a spur to the east and is reached after a 15-minute descent off the main range. It makes a pleasant place to pass the night, or can be bypassed in favour of the new Arete Biv.

Back up on Dundas Ridge, more undulating travel follows, with a gradual climb to Logan, then a more significant climb to Dundas (1500 m), whose top is covered with a large trig station. From a knob just southwest of Dundas, an unmarked and unmaintained route descends to the Mangahao Valley over Triangle Knob, presenting a possible bad-weather escape route off the tops.

Beyond Dundas, travel proves mostly undulating. About 30 metres below the top of Pt 1434, sidle left to a narrow cairned track leading across rock and tussock faces to Arete Biv.

The biv commands one of the best 'tops' positions of any hut in the Tararuas, and the small red shelter seems fittingly tiny in the gold tussock landscape. From the hut, the nearby Twins and Bannister look rather fearsome, while Mitre, Girdlestone and Brockett form significant summits to the southeast. Built in 2007, the new two-bunk hut is a welcome replacement for the old damp biv, and is located on a new site approximately 200 metres to the south (grid reference: 158-480).

Gentians – one of the last alpine plants to flower in summer

From the hut, pass a sizeable tarn, and then climb tussock slopes up to the summit of Arete (1505 m). This and the next peak, Pukematawai, are interesting because together they lie at the head of virtually all of the major Tararua rivers: the Waiohine, Waingawa, Mangahao, Otaki and Ruamahanga. There are good views from here of the U-shaped Park valley, which Leslie Adkin first proposed had glacial origins. While the Park's profile certainly seems to suggest that glaciers did shape it, a lack of moraines normally associated with glaciation raises some doubts about the theory.

There's a track junction just southeast of Pukematawai, marked by several poles, where the main range route continues. Instead, head right here onto a prominent spur that forms a crooked route to the scrubline, past a signposted turn-off to Girdlestone Saddle and eventually to Te Matawai Hut. This rather unusual hut, which seems to be a tribute to the worst of 1970s architecture, recently had its high ceiling lowered, making it warmer than it used to be. A covered veranda makes a good spot to enjoy the sunrise and a morning brew.

The final leg of the tramp follows a prominent largely forested ridge over the summits of Richards Knob (past the Gable End Ridge turn-off), Twin Peak (where there's a trig and another cross), and finally Waiopehu. While you can see over the scrub that grows on these knobs, they are no longer covered with the *Celmisia spectabilis* daisies that were photographed by Adkin early in the 20th century – perhaps this is a sign of rising scrublines.

A short distance down from the summit of Waiopehu, just through a small patch of beech forest, is the new Waiopehu Hut, built in March–April 2002 and sporting panoramic views over the Manawatu. It replaces the old Waiopehu Hut, now removed, which was located a short distance down the ridge.

The final romp down the ridge passes through beech forest at first, then kamahi-tawa-podocarp forest with some extensive sections of tree ferns. It's further than you might expect and can be muddy, but eventually you reach farmland, from where it's a flat stroll to the carpark on Poads Road. By the end you'll be feeling the effects – and satisfaction – of having crossed the Tararua Range.

Tramper heading from Ruapae to East Peak

Mangahao Flats

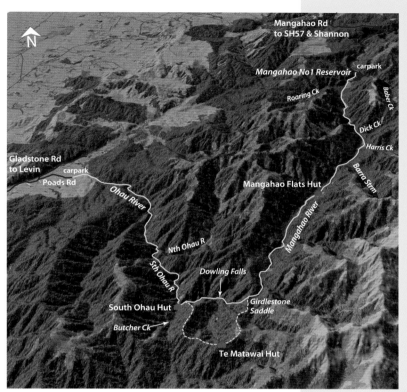

Duration 2 days

Grade Medium

Times Mangahao No. 1 Reservoir to Mangahao Flats Hut (16 bunks, woodstove, $5/night): 5–6 hours. Mangahao Flats Hut to Girdlestone Saddle: 3 hours. Girdlestone Saddle to South Ohau Hut (10 bunks, woodstove, $5/night): 1–2 hours. South Ohau River to Poads Road: 3–4 hours.

Maps S25 Levin, Tararua Forest Park Map

Access Turn off SH 57 at Shannon onto Mangahao Road and follow this until its end at the Mangahao No. 1 Reservoir and dam. It's a long, narrow, winding metalled road. The tramp ends at Poads Road, which is accessible off SH 57 at Levin on Tararua, Gladstone and Poads roads.

Alternative Route For those who want to go only as far as Mangahao Flats and back, it's possible to end the tramp slightly differently. Downstream of Harris Creek, travel up Dick Creek, over a small bush saddle, and then down Baber Creek, to emerge on the Puketurua Track, which ends at the far side of the dam. This is, however, off-track travel and is classed as medium–hard.

Information DOC Kapiti Area Office, Ph 04 296 1112

The Mangahao is undoubtedly one of the most attractive rivers in Tararua Forest Park, and a tramp to Mangahao Flats Hut provides a good weekend trip for moderately experienced trampers. From the head of the Mangahao, it's also possible for more experienced trampers to continue over Girdlestone Saddle into the Ohau catchment.

After the long drive in from Shannon, you're more than ready to get out and stretch your legs. There's an impressive dam here, one of the earliest ones built in the country. Suggestions that the Mangahao had potential for generating hydro-electricity were mooted as far back as 1911, and the resultant dams were completed in 1924. Until recently, much of the reservoir was filled with the ugly stumps of trees that were drowned when the valley was flooded, but these have since been removed, and the area is more appealing as a result.

The track starts right from the reservoir edge and immediately plunges into bush, crossing a swingbridge over an unnamed creek after 10 minutes. However, when the reservoir is not full, it's often easier to sidle around its silty edge.

Tramper overlooks pool in Mangahao River

On a fine day when river levels are normal, parties may wish to avoid the track altogether and instead amble up-river. The track itself – typically for a Tararua valley sidle – has considerable up and down, especially in the first section to Harris Creek. In contrast, boulder-hopping along the river proves a delight, with frequent opportunities for swimming in deep green pools. After about an hour you reach a swingbridge, where the track crosses to the true right of the valley.

If you are following the river, there's a section of gorge travel upstream of the bridge. While this is not difficult, you will need to swim in a few very deep pools unless you scramble around in the bush. Be aware, however, that floods can change this section of river considerably, and if you are in any doubt it's best to stick to the track. Even the track requires some caution where recent storms have caused damage. After crossing Dick Creek, the track follows bush terraces for 10 minutes to emerge at Harris Creek. The old Harris Creek Hut that had existed here since 1977 was removed in 2003. Up-valley there is good river travel once again as far as Mangahao Flats, making a dry-weather alternative to the track.

The track from Harris Creek bridge is also fairly pleasant, with considerably less up and down than the previous section. Thirty minutes later you reach the other major sidestream in the valley, the Barra. In flood, the Barra often used to be impassable, but in 2003 DOC erected a new bridge. Aside from a couple of side streams (including the Roaring Creek) which can be problematic in flood, the entire route as far as Mangahao Flats is feasible in all but the worst weather.

Beyond Barra Stream, the track crosses a slip, where there are clear views over the Mangahao River as it curls around a substantial horseshoe bend. Not far beyond, you reach Mangahao Flats Hut situated on a bush terrace above the river. The large, roomy, 16-bunk hut was built in 1992 as a replacement for the old Avalanche Flats Hut.

After a night at Mangahao Flats Hut, most parties choose simply to walk back down the valley, but those who have made suitable transport arrangements can opt instead to continue into the Ohau Valley over Girdlestone Saddle. This section, however, is more difficult and can only be achieved when river levels are low. From the hut, a track continues up-valley on the true right. It passes through a couple of interesting 'frost flats' where stunted manuka grows, while further up are some larger grassy flats ideal for camping.

The track eventually crosses the Mangahao at a prominent river fork, then sidles through beech forest for10 minutes. Once over a stream it begins the short five-minute climb to Girdlestone Saddle and a track intersection. One track leads off up a bush spur towards Te Matawai Hut, while the other heads across the saddle down to the South Ohau River. Unless wet weather threatens, take the latter option, which soon drops into a small, steep creek. A violent flood has severely damaged this creek, and you'll need to do a bit of scrambling over loose rock and log debris. This doesn't last long, however, before a well-marked sidle track takes you out of the creek on the true left to bypass Dowling Falls.

This track soon deposits you in the South Ohau River, which you follow downstream to the junction with Butchers Stream. The old South Ohau Hut was removed in 2003 after an earthquake undermined it, and DOC replaced it with a new 10-bunk hut at an adjacent site in May 2008. Travel down the Ohau from this point proves fairly straightforward, despite the gorge marked on the map – in recent years this has been substantially filled in with gravel from floods. It takes a further 1.5 hours to reach the confluence with the North Ohau River.

After a further half-hour in the river, a well-benched track starts on the true left. It passes the site of the old Ohau Shelter (which is now a good camping spot) then crosses a footbridge and sidles down valley. By this stage the forest is almost subtropical, with nikau palms, mahoe, kiekie vines and dense tangles of supplejack, through which the track passes on an easy gradient. After crossing another footbridge you emerge suddenly onto farmland, from where it's a 15-minute walk to the carpark on Poads Road. Please respect this private land by sticking to the track, as future access depends on the goodwill of the farmers.

Dragonfly, Ohau Valley

Mitre Flats

Duration 2–3 days

Grade Medium

Times Upper Waingawa Road to Mitre Flats Hut (15 bunks, wood-stove, gas rings, $15/night): 3–3.5 hours. Mitre Flats Hut to Mitre: ascent 3 hours; descent 2 hours.

Maps S26 Carterton, S25 Levin, Tararua Forest Parkmap

Access Turn off the SH 2 Masterton bypass onto Upper Plain Road and follow this for some 10 km before turning left onto Upper Waingawa Road. There's an area to park your car at the farm roadend, known as 'The Pines'.

Alternative Route From the summit of Mitre, it's possible to traverse Girdlestone and The Three Kings, then drop down over Baldy back to Mitre Flats Hut. This is, however, a very long day suitable only for experienced trampers.

Information DOC Wairarapa Area Office, Ph 06 377 0700

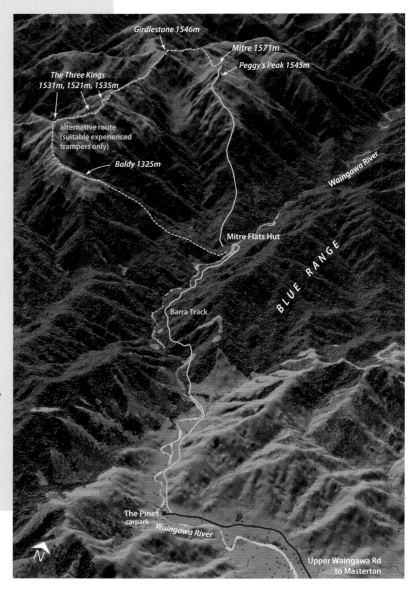

The Waingawa is one the principal rivers of the eastern side of the Tararua Range, draining the slopes of the highest peak in the park, Mitre. At 1571 metres, Mitre is hardly a giant – even by North Island standards – but the tramp to the top is worthwhile, with some good views and a comfortable hut en route.

From 'The Pines', follow a 4WD farm track for some distance, to where poles lead down onto river terraces of the Waingawa. Shortly afterwards, a track starts through regenerating bush and finally leads into mature forest at the boundary of Tararua Forest Park. You are now on the benched Barra Track, named after Tararua veteran Bert Barra, who was something of a local hunting legend. He spent his last days living in a hut overlooking the Waingawa River. In places the track sidles quite high above the river, although you're often within earshot of it rushing through gorges below. The forest is a combination of rimu, kamahi and supplejack with some beech, and at its densest these form quite a dark canopy over the trail. During summer, the northern rata flowers spectacularly, a tribute to DOC's ongoing possum control in the area.

Several viewpoints open out, mainly of the river, but on one occasion you can see Jumbo and even Jumbo Hut. Later comes a view of Mitre itself. Soon after glimpsing Mitre Flats Hut, the track drops down to cross a new footbridge (built in 2004), happily avoiding a climb around a slip that used to tax trampers and hunters alike.

The current 14-bunk hut (completed in 1988) is the third that has occupied Mitre Flats; the original was built in 1933 from timber cut on site and iron cladding carried in on horseback. The second hut, constructed in 1953 by the Masterton YMCA, required two loads of materials to be lugged in as, heartbreakingly, the first load was mostly washed away in one of the Waingawa's notorious floods. Although today's hut is a pleasant and popular place to spend the night, those who prefer camping can find plenty of secluded spots on the northern end of the flats.

Tramper on Peggy's Peak, Tararua Forest Park

The track to Mitre starts near the hut, at first climbing stiffly onto a ridge, from where the gradient eases. Then it's a steady uphill plod, surprisingly without any really steep sections. Initially there's a rich understorey of kidney ferns beneath a canopy of rimu, miro

South Mitre Stream, Tararua Forest Park

and kamahi, but these later lapse into silver beech. Typically for the Tararuas, the silver beech becomes more and more stunted as you gain altitude, often forming exquisitely twisted shapes, until finally a band of leatherwood takes over. Above the scrub band, rock cairns lead ever upwards over tussock and scree slopes, and there are increasingly good views of the Kings, Baldy and the upper reaches of the Waingawa. The first summit reached is Peggy's Peak, which is separated from nearby Mitre by just a short and narrow stretch of ridge. Fortunately, the often strong winds that blow here come mainly from the west, thus pushing you away from a steep drop-off overhanging the South Mitre Stream.

A large cairn marks the summit of Mitre, the top of the Tararuas, which is flat enough to support several tramping parties at once. There are views of Dundas Ridge and the spectacularly nasty-looking Bannister to the north, undulating Tarn Ridge to the northwest, and endless other forested slopes surrounding them. Even Kapiti Island is sometimes visible, far off in the haze.

The descent back to Mitre Flats is surprisingly non-jarring for a 1200-metre drop, mainly because the ridge reclines at such an even gradient. It's perfectly feasible to climb Mitre and walk back out in one day, but if there's no hurry another night at Mitre Flats could be pleasant. An extra day allows you time to follow the river back to the carpark. Although there are several gorges along the way, there is only one real significant swim near the end, and that can be avoided by scrambling out on the true left bank to rejoin the track.

Mt Holdsworth & Jumbo

Duration 2 days

Grade Medium

Times Holdsworth Lodge to Powell Hut (32 bunks, gas rings and heater,$15/ night): 3–4 hours. Powell to Jumbo Hut (20 bunks, gas rings, wood-stove, $15/ night): 2.5–3.5 hours. Jumbo to Atiwhakatu Hut (8 bunks, open fire, $5/night): 1.5 hours. Atiwhakatu to Holdsworth Lodge: 2–3 hours.

Maps S26 Carterton, S25 Levin, Tararua Forest Parkmap

Access From SH 2, just south of Masterton, turn onto Norfolk Road; this eventually becomes Mt Holdsworth Road. At the roadend is a large carpark, toilets and Holdsworth Lodge (which is available for overnight stays).

Alternative Route If the weather is bad, it's possible to drop off the ridge north of Mt Holdsworth along a spur known as the East Holdsworth Ridge. This joins the Atiwhakatu Valley track at the Holdsworth Creek confluence.

Information DOC Wairarapa Area Office, Ph 06 377 0700

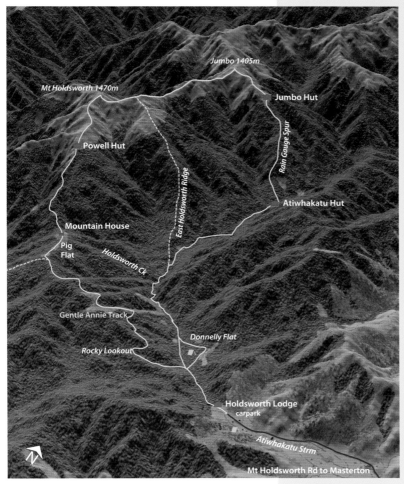

This route – up to Powell Hut and Mt Holdsworth, then across the tops to Jumbo Hut, and finally down the Atiwhakatu Valley – forms one of the classic Tararua weekend tramps, with the bonus that it is a tidy round trip. It's enjoyable no matter what the time of year, but be warned: on weekends and during summer, expect crowds! Powell Hut has, for some years, been the most popular hut in the park and regularly gets full. Although this is classed as a medium trip, the tops – like most of those in the

Tararuas – are extremely exposed and can be lethal for ill-equipped or inexperienced parties during bad weather.

From Holdsworth Lodge (where there is an intentions book) a gravelled track heads up-valley, soon crossing the Atiwhakatu River on a sizeable footbridge. Shortly afterwards, the track forks; head left here up the well-benched and gravelled Gentle Annie Track, which has

Silver beech forest, Mt Holdsworth track

been upgraded in recent years. At first, some Tararua stalwarts bemoaned these improvements, but in reality a track as popular as this one needs a fairly hardened surface if it is to avoid becoming severely eroded. As you climb, the vegetation changes gradually from a mix of the more lush podocarp-broadleaf-beech forest to one that is increasingly dominated by beech, mainly silver.

After steady upwards progress, a flatter section of the track leads onto a viewpoint at Rocky Lookout. Undulating ridge travel ensues, until you reach a prominent junction where a track branches off down to Totara Flats. More undulating tramping leads across Pig Flat until at the end you reach the three-sided Mountain House Shelter, built by the Wellington Tramping and Mountaineering Club to replace their old hut called Mountain House.

Beyond the shelter, the track steepens for the final push to Powell Hut, which sits on the bushline. This modern, large, well-designed hut was officially opened in 2000, the most recent in a succession of Powell Huts dating back to 1939. Previous versions were reputedly haunted by 'Cedric the Ghost', thought to be the spirit of hunter Cedric Wilson, who died near Mitre during 1945. It seems Cedric has sensibly avoided taking up residence in the new hut.

With its commanding views over the Wairarapa plains and the Atiwhakatu Valley, the veranda of Powell Hut is a fine place to watch the last of the day's light fade, followed later by the twinkling emergence of both the stars and the lights of Masterton. Above Powell Hut, a well-worn (but not poled) route leads up to Mt Holdsworth (1470 m), the most popular summit in the Tararua Range. A trig station marks the top, which – more often than not – is shrouded in cloud.

Drop down onto the ridge leading north to Jumbo in the direction indicated by the signpost. The well-traipsed tops here are pretty easy going by Tararua standards, dropping steadily to a low saddle and then beginning a climb up past a tarn towards the angular summit of Jumbo. On a good day there are views of the Broken Axe Pinnacles, McGregor and Baldy. Near Jumbo a signpost indicates the correct spur to follow down to Jumbo Hut. Like Powell, Jumbo Hut also commands a fine position on the bushline, with extensive views eastwards.

A well-marked track leads from Jumbo down into the Atiwhakatu Valley on what is called 'Rain Gauge Spur' – a once unofficial route (starting beyond the rain gauge) that is now more popular than the older track further north. After a sharp descent, the track reaches the Atiwhakatu River just upstream of Atiwhakatu Hut.

From the hut you head downstream on a well-benched and graded track – a far cry from the rough old route that used to exist. Now that all the major side streams have been bridged, this is an all-weather track. Fast travel leads onto Holdsworth Creek, spanned by a swingbridge. Shortly before Donnelly Flat the track has been upgraded and now includes an extensive section of boardwalk. Donnelly Flat offers good camping spots, complete with permanent fireplaces. From here it's simply a matter of ambling back out to Holdsworth Lodge.

Powell Hut, Mt Holdsworth

Southern Crossing

Duration 2–3 days

Grade Medium–Hard

Times Otaki Forks to Field Hut (20 bunks, wood-stove, $5/night): 2–3 hours. Field Hut to Kime Hut (20 bunks, $5/night): 2–3 hours. Kime to Alpha Hut (20 bunks, wood-stove, $5/night): 4–5 hours. Alpha to Kaitoke via Marchant Ridge: 6–8 hours; via Tauherenikau Valley and Smith Creek: 7–8 hours.

Maps S26 Carterton, Tararua Forest Park Map

Access From SH 1, just south of Otaki, turn off onto Otaki Gorge Road and follow it for 19 km. Before the end of the road there's a large carpark, toilets, a caretaker's residence and access to Parawai Lodge. The tramp concludes at a large gravel carpark at the end of Marchant Road, off SH 2 at Kaitoke about 14 km north of Upper Hutt. Owing to vandalism, it is not recommended that you park a car overnight at the Kaitoke end.

Alternative Route From Alpha Hut it's possible to complete the more traditional Southern Crossing over Bull Mound to Cone Hut and from there to the roadend at Walls Whare.

Information DOC Kapiti Area Office, Ph 04 296 1112; DOC Wairarapa Area Office, 06 377 0700.

Perhaps *the* classic Tararua tramp is the Southern Crossing. It's a track with a long history, preceding even the formation of New Zealand's first tramping club, the Tararua Tramping Club, in 1919. The idea for what later became known as the Southern Crossing originated with the Mt Hector Track Committee, a group that sought to develop a tourist track in the southern Tararuas during the first part of the 20th century. The group erected three huts: Alpha (built in 1915 and the first alpine hut in the Tararua Range), Top Tauherenikau (built in 1917) and Te Moemoea Hut (built in 1919 near Otaki Forks).

The original Southern Crossing route used to finish (or begin) at Walls Whare, near

Greytown, but most parties now opt to end at Kaitoke, near Upper Hutt. It's somewhat ironic that this route is not actually a crossing and does in fact start and finish on the western side of the Tararua Range. That said, ending at Kaitoke allows for somewhat easier transport arrangements, particularly for Wellington trampers.

The starting point, Otaki Forks, lies at the junction of several rivers and tracks, and forms a popular area for camping and picnicking as well as tramping. From the overnight parking area, a short track leads down to a picnic spot where a substantial new footbridge spans the Waiotauru River. Across the bridge, a brief climb leads to a grassy river terrace and a junction with the track to Waitewaewae. Take the track signposted to Field Hut. A long but not particularly strenuous ascent ensues.

The track initially passes through regenerating scrub, then soon enters more mature forest where kamahi and hinau dominate, along with the occasional totara. Typically for the Tararuas, silver beech takes over higher up. Further on, you reach Field Hut, the oldest-surviving hut in the park. Commissioned by the Tararua Tramping Club and completed in 1924, Field Hut was built out of timber pit-sawn on site by master bushman Joe Gibbs. Although the hut has changed extensively since then, it's still just as welcome today as it must have been for those early trampers. Many parties opt to walk this far on their first night, in order to break up the long climb to Kime Hut.

Above Field Hut and after a brief climb through subalpine scrub, you reach the aptly named Table Top – a flat expanse of tops now partially boardwalked. As is usual on Tararua tops, there are very few poles, but the track is certainly well-defined from years of use. A few sections sidle, but mostly the route just heads uphill. Botanically, the area proves quite lush, with gentians, North Island edelweiss, several *Celmisia* species and the attractive but

Evening light on the Tararua Range from Bridge Peak

uncharacteristically soft-spined Tararua speargrass. Near the top, some waratahs appear, and shortly after comes the signpost indicating the turn-off to Bridge Peak and Maungahuka Hut. Not far from here, just over the gentle rise of Hut Mound, Kime Hut lies nestled in a shallow dip by a prominent tarn.

Kime Hut

Due to its large size and high ceiling, Kime can be a cold hut, and – as often as not – the weather is bleak. However, the hut has recently had new mattresses installed, making it more comfortable than it used to be. From here you embark across an exposed section of tops to Alpha Hut. During bad weather, particularly a howling southerly, parties should opt to stay put and wait for a clearance before attempting it. Poles have recently been positioned at key places between Kime and Alpha huts, making navigation in poor conditions easier on the sections where topography loses definition.

Initially, the track climbs to Field Peak, then drops sharply to a saddle, then climbs again to Mt Hector, at 1529 metres the highest point on the crossing. On a good day, Mt Hector provides a remarkable viewpoint, with mountains as distant as the Inland Kaikoura Range sometimes visible. Marking the summit is a substantial wooden cross, built to commemorate trampers and climbers who lost their lives in both world wars. In winter, windblown sastrugi-like ice sometimes lends it more the appearance of a memorial to Antarctic explorers.

From Mt Hector the route heads almost directly south, dropping to a shallow saddle, before climbing over the mounds known as The Beehives. The narrowest section of the entire route ensues, one that could potentially be dangerous in high winds or winter conditions.

Beyond, undulating tops travel leads to Atkinson, which is marked by a short waratah. Past Pt 1372 the terrain becomes very flat and almost moorlike, but the track is so well-defined that it would be difficult to come off it anywhere – except, of course, when it lies under a covering of snow. From Aston, the track starts curling southeast, around the Dress Circle and then begins a climb onto Alpha, where it swings directly east. On a good day, Alpha affords perhaps the best vantage point of the crossing, with views back around the sweep of the Dress Circle and over the extensive forests of the neighbouring Tauherenikau and Hutt catchments.

A steady plod from Alpha takes you once more down into forest, from where it's a pleasant stroll through wonderfully stunted silver beech to Alpha Hut. This version is the third Alpha, built in 1983. Beyond Alpha, a forested track leads towards the Marchant Ridge and a choice of routes out. After passing Hells Gate (a small dip in the bush ridge with an exaggerated name) you reach a track junction. The left branch would take you over Bull Mound and out to Walls Whare via Mt Reeves – the traditional Southern Crossing route. Instead, head right here, over Omega, and continue along the undulating forest of Marchant Ridge until you reach the signposted junction with the Block XVI Track.

There's another choice of routes here: either the fairly tedious up-and-down of the deceptively long Marchant Ridge; or the option that it is preferred by many, out through the Tauherenikau Valley via the Block XVI Track. (Both routes eventually rejoin near the track end at Kaitoke.) The latter does involve a 300-metre descent, but once you are down in the Tauherenikau Valley, travel is generally flat and easygoing on forested river terraces that are dominated by extensive stands of rimu. Past Smith Creek Shelter, an agreeably shady and well-benched track ascends gradually beside Smith Creek, broken only by one scramble around an area of slips. Near the head of Smith Creek, the track climbs more sharply over a saddle of regenerating forest to begin a sidle towards Kaitoke, passing the Marchant Ridge track en route. At the end of the tramp you will feel that you have really covered some ground – which you have. It's somewhat deflating then, to hear that the fastest time for completing the annual run along the entire Southern Crossing is an astonishing four hours and 27 minutes!

Dress Circle and Southern Crossing from near Alpha

Otaki River Gorge

Duration 2 days

Grade Hard. Although this is a relatively easy trip in good conditions, there are no easy ways to escape the river. Flood conditions make it impossible or very dangerous.

Times Otaki Forks to Waitewaewae Hut (16 bunks, wood-stove, $5/night): 6 hours. Waitewaewae Hut to Otaki Forks via Otaki River Gorge: 8–12 hours depending on current.

Maps S26 Carterton, Tararua Parkmap

Access Just south of Otaki, turn off SH 1 onto Otaki Gorge Road and follow it for about 19 km. Before the end of the road there's a large carpark, toilets, a caretaker's residence and access to Parawai Lodge.

Alternative Route By walking to Penn Creek Hut (6 bunks, open fire, $5/night) via Field Hut and Table Top, and joining the Otaki River at the Penn Creek confluence, trampers could tube just the lower section of the river.

Information DOC Kapiti Area Office, Ph 04 296 1112

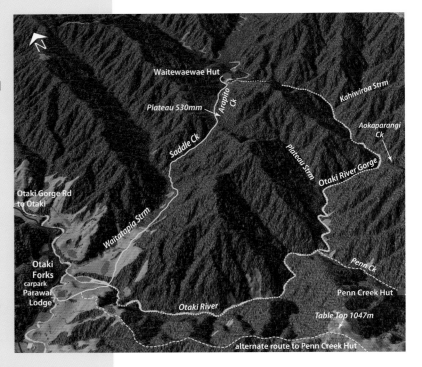

On account of its unpredictable and tempestuous climate, the Tararua Range gets a fair amount of negative press, even from those who fiercely love the place. But no one can deny the singular attribute of Tararua Forest Park that sets it out from virtually any other tramping ground in the country – its wonderful gorges. Plenty of back-country valleys, notably on the West Coast, bristle with often-fearsome gorges, but none can match the Tararuas for its sheer number of easily floatable, tramper-friendly watercourses. Virtually every major river in the park – the Mangahao, Waingawa, Waiohine, Ruamahanga, and Tauherenikau – boasts at least one decent section of gorge, but there's possibly no better weekend gorge adventure than the Otaki.

A word of caution: tubing the Otaki River should only be attempted by experienced parties and capable swimmers, and even then only during summer or early autumn when water temperatures are at their peak. Under no circumstances attempt the trip after heavy rain or on a poor forecast. The trip involves walking from Otaki Forks into Waitewaewae

Hut for the night, then tubing down the Otaki back to the Forks. While there are a few places to escape the river, be aware that once you start down the Otaki, you're pretty much committed.

Tubing involves a bit more gear than your average tramping trip: tubes for a start. The best tubes are 20-inch (60 cm) truck tyre tubes. These can be procured from a friendly garage or tyre store, but ask well in advance so they can set aside some for you. Pumped to a perfection of buoyancy, these tubes have enough room to plant your bum in the middle, rest your pack on the back, and drape your feet in a downstream direction. Take a spare tube or two, a puncture repair kit, spare valves, and a reliable pump.

Wetsuits are essential and you should wear a helmet as well (a rafting one is best, but a climbing or cycling helmet will suffice). It's also worth taking dry bags for cameras, spare clothes and food – fairly inexpensive, pack liner-size dry bags are now available. Even during summer, trampers can get dangerously cold by spending all day in the river. So take and eat plenty of snack food, stop to warm up or brew up in the sun, and consider walking gravelly sections to get the blood flowing again.

From the overnight parking area at Otaki Forks, a short track leads down to a grassy picnic spot where a substantial footbridge spans the Waiotauru River. Across the bridge, a brief climb leads to a grassy river terrace and a track junction. Ignore the track signposted to Field Hut, and take the one indicating Waitewaewae Hut. After sidling the grassy terrace for a bit, the track descends to a long swingbridge over the substantial volume of the Otaki River. You'll exit the river about 100 metres upstream, so this makes a good place from which to gauge the colour and depth of the water.

The next part of the tramp essentially follows an old tramline built for extracting

Upper Otaki River, Tararua Forest Park

timber logs during the 1930s. At one point there is a partially restored section of rail, and at another the hulking form of an old steam-driven traction engine. Shortly beyond, the track begins an ascent up Saddle Creek through lush forest with a dense understorey of tree ferns. An eroded section of track climbs steeply up the final pinch onto the Plateau (530 m), where the track flattens out – but can be muddy. A short descent beside Arapito Creek brings you to a junction.

Near here the Otaki River makes a large sweeping curve. When river levels allow, the quickest route to Waitewaewae Hut involves descending the informal track beside the remainder of Arapito Creek, then heading up the Otaki River for 15 minutes or so (wading is required for a few sections). Otherwise it's a fairly tedious climb and sidle above a substantial slip on the track around the bend.

Waitewaewae Hut commands a bush terrace, set back from the Otaki River, where a few podocarps emerge through the otherwise beech-dominant forest. After a night at the large and functional hut, you're ready for the main adventure: tubing the Otaki.

Making your way back down-river around the big bend will give you the opportunity to assess river conditions. A short distance downstream of Arapito Creek is the first of many long deep pools in this section of the river. Here, beech forest arches over the banks and the river flows softly between the greywacke boulders in an unhurried way.

The first half of the river is the most heavily gorged and features the most rapids. When the current proves sufficient, tubing makes a supremely sensible way of travelling downstream. However after an extremely dry period, when the Otaki becomes very low, the flat sections offer precious little current and you may have to paddle.

Mostly the rapids are easy Grade 1 cascades. There is a certain excitement as the current quickens, pulling you downwards into the maw of whitewater, then spitting you out the bottom – sometimes even on your tube. Keeping your feet pointed downstream enables you to kick off any boulders. All of the rapids can be tubed, although one chute has a drop of over 1.5 metres and those in doubt may want to portage it. Be aware however, that floods can change the nature of the river, so if in doubt, scout ahead on foot before running a questionable rapid.

Mostly the Otaki is an enclosed world of river, rock and overhanging greenery, although at one point the valley offers a memorable glimpse of the Tararua Peaks, two green pyramids high above on the main Tararua Range.

At least one person in your party should have the task of counting off the main tributaries, so you can estimate progress on the map. Kahiwiroa Stream, Aokaparangi Creek and Plateau Stream come first. Beyond, the river opens out somewhat, and a few gravelly sections offer the opportunity to walk – which can be faster and warmer than floating.

Lower down, below most of the real gorges, Penn Creek spills in on the true left. This major tributary of the Otaki offers an escape route, leading up Penn Creek to Penn Creek Hut where a good track leads over Table Top, past Field Hut and down to Otaki Forks. Alternatively, some parties have escaped up Plateau Stream and intercepted the Waitewaewae Track.

Past the Penn Creek confluence, the Otaki River becomes rather sedate, with fewer rapids. Further downstream you can see the enormous slips that have ravaged the lower section of the valley in recent years.

As the Otaki curls around a final bend, the long swingbridge comes into sight. Exit the river about 100 metres upstream of the bridge, where a short track climbs the bank to rejoin your inward track. No matter how enjoyable the tubing has been, you're probably fairly pleased to see the end by now, and grateful for the opportunity to walk the short distance back to the carpark, even though at first you are likely to be a little wobbly on your feet.

Tubing a rapid on the Otaki River, Tararua Forest Park

Mt Matthews

Duration 1–2 days

Grade Medium

Times Visitor centre to Turere bridge: 1.5–2 hours. Orongorongo River to Matthews Stream: 1 hour. Matthews Stream to Mt Matthews: 2–3 hours each way.

Maps Wellington R27/28

Access North of Wellington on SH 2, take the Petone off-ramp, follow signs to Wainui-omata, then head south along the Coast Road. After about 10 km a signpost indicates the turn-off to the Catchpool Valley. The roadend is about 2 km further on at the large Catchpool carpark, where there are toilets and information panels. Note that the gates at the Coast Road entrance into the Catchpool Valley close at dusk and reopen at 8 a.m.

Alternative Route An alternative route up Mt Matthews can be taken from the Wairarapa side, up Mukamuka Stream onto the South Saddle, and then up to the summit itself. Access for this route is from Palliser Bay, west of Lake Ferry.

Huts & Camps Jans, Shamrock, Raukawa, Haurangi and Oaks huts are available for booking (book on-line at www.doc.govt.nz). The huts have mattresses, cooking facilities, plates, cups and utensils and cost between $54 and $135 per night, depending on season and bunk capacity. Camping is possible at several sites in the Orongorongo Valley (at Manuka Flat and Big Bend) and near Matthews Stream.

Information DOC Wellington Visitor Centre, Ph 04 384 7770

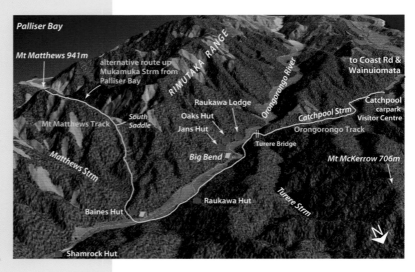

The relatively low, but deceptively rugged Rimutakas are the southernmost range along the North Island's mountain spine, which extends from East Cape to Wellington. Ascending Mt Matthews, which at 941 metres is the highest peak in the range, can be accomplished over a weekend, or if you're really keen, in as little as one day.

Access to the peak is on one of the country's most popular walks, the Orongorongo Track. This track departs from the Catchpool carpark (note that the Catchpool Visitor Centre has closed).

The gentle gradient of the Orongorongo Track passes through an area of recently felled pine forest at first, then heads into a semi-tropical grove where nikau palms and kiekie vines are conspicuous, before breaking out into a more open area of red beech forest. Later, there are pockets of rimu, miro and kamahi. Attractive information panels provide details of the area's ecology. A bad storm wiped out many of the track's footbridges in March 2005 but these have all since been replaced. After about 5 kilometres, the track descends to an arched bridge over the Turere Stream and finally into the gravelly expanse of the Orongorongo River itself. The Orongorongo is the largest watercourse in the park and runs southward to meet Cook Strait on the coastline separating Wellington from the Wairarapa.

There are several DOC-managed huts in the valley, which due to their popularity must be pre-booked. Numerous private huts also lie tucked away in the bush, dating back to the days before the formation of the Rimutaka Forest Park, when the valley was a popular spot for Wellingtonians to build holiday baches. The track to Mt Matthews starts about 3 kilometres upstream of the Turere footbridge. Trampers can reach it either on the Big Bend Track on the true right of the valley, or – if water levels are low – on the faster route along the riverbed.

There are good views of the range from the open riverbed, although Mt Matthews as yet remains hidden. Emergent above the forest are numerous northern rata trees, many of which sadly have been devastated by possums, first introduced to New Zealand in the Rimutaka Range in 1893. With such a long history of being browsed, the Rimutaka forests have very visible scars. Erosion remains prominent, both from goat browsing and the devastation wrought by the 1968 storm that sank the *Wahine*.

After an hour's walk up-valley you reach a signpost on the true left of the river indicating the start of the Mt Matthews track. The track soon passes a small clearing where the Hutt Valley Tramping Club's Baines Hut is situated. (Due to river erosion, the club plans to remove the hut.) Beyond, the track leads into Matthews Stream, crossing it a few times. If you have any doubts about the power of the Earth to thrust mountains up along geological faults, the next section of track soon dispels them. Typical of mountain ranges in the North Island, the Rimutaka Range is composed chiefly of greywacke and has been uplifted over the last 12 million years. Much of this uplift has occurred slowly, at the rate

Orongorongo Valley, Rimutaka Range beyond

of a few centimetres per year, but on occasions severe earthquakes have made dramatic upthrusts. The last major local earthquake occurred in 1855, measured about 8.0 on the Richter scale and raised the Rimutaka Range by approximately 3 metres. Some of the large eroded scars on the range were also caused by the quake. The track climbs very steeply over this landscape through open beech forest, then it sidles across a bush-covered knob before reaching a signpost. Here the side track to the South Saddle branches off.

The main track leads uphill again, and after a breathless ascent it emerges onto a grassy plateau. Impressive views unfold westwards of Wellington Harbour and the surrounding hills, while to the east you can hear the pounding surf of Palliser Bay.

The last section of the climb leads up a very steep face, onto a narrow section of ridge cloaked in silver beech forest. The trees form uniform stands here as well as in the Tararua Range further north, and are often gnarled and heavily moss-clad. Through this forest a deceptively long (though well-marked) route leads along the ridge, dipping down to the right at one point, before finally reaching Mt Matthews itself. Disappointingly (for the views), the summit is forest-clad, but gaps in the trees allow glimpses of the long curve of Palliser Bay and of the Wairarapa plains below.

The trip back to your camp needs to be done carefully to avoid wrenching your knees – hold on to the tree trunks to help brake your descent. Whiteheads and riflemen are common in these higher altitudes of the park, and you may see flocks of them flitting over branches in their search for insects.

Silver beech forest, Rimutaka Range

Washpool Hut

Duration 2 days

Grade Medium

Times Putangirua Pinnacles campsite to Washpool Hut (6 bunks, wood-stove, $5/night): 4–5 hours. Washpool Hut to Whatarangi road via Makotukutuku Stream (Washpool Creek): 3–4 hours.

Map S28 Palliser

Access From Featherston turn off SH 2 onto SH 63 and drive to Martinborough. Head south on the Martinborough–Pirinoa Road, which eventually becomes Whangamoana and Whatarangi roads. Thirteen kilometres past the Lake Ferry turnoff, just past where the road first hugs the coastline, is Te Kopi. After a further 500 metres, a signposted road branches off to the camping area and carpark at Putangirua Pinnacles Scenic Reserve. Allow an hour to drive from Martinborough.

Alternative Route From Washpool Hut you can extend your tramp by taking a steepish track (2.5–3.5 hours) to Pararaki Hut (6 bunks, open fire, $5/night), where it is possible to follow the Pararaki Stream down to the road (3.5–4 hours).

Accommodation The Putangirua Pinnacles campsite ($5/person) has water and toilets. Trampers may consider booking the former ranger base at nearby Te Kopi, now a lodge with space for 10 people.

Information DOC Wairarapa Area Office, 06 377 0700

Some tramping areas are neglected, not because they don't have anything to offer, but simply because they are overshadowed by better-known areas nearby. The Wairarapa's Aorangi Range is a case in point: although hunters frequent the park, it's often overlooked by trampers who instead flock – in increasing numbers – to the adjacent Tararua Range.

Situated in the southern Wairarapa, the 19,380-hectare Aorangi Forest Park (formerly known as Haurangi Forest Park) has eight huts, plus two lodges, and a small network of tracks. Its easterly position means the range often experiences dry – if windy – weather when nor' westers are soaking the Tararuas.

This tramp into Washpool Hut is arguably the most interesting of several weekend tramps possible in the park, combining some ridge travel, some river travel, and the added bonus of starting at perhaps the Wairarapa's most bizarre landforms: the Putangirua Pinnacles.

The tramp begins at a campground in the

Putangirua Pinnacles Scenic Reserve, near the edge of Palliser Bay, and ends where the Makotukutuku Stream (also known as Washpool Creek) intercepts Whatarangi Road, about six kilometres apart. A bike makes a handy alternative to arranging a car shuffle. You'll need permission from the farmer to walk down the stream through farmland (contact DOC for details).

From the carpark at the camping area, follow the marker poles up the gravelly riverbed of the Putangirua Stream, which at this point has little to suggest the wonders that lie up-valley. After 15 minutes, pass the signposted turnoff to the Bush Walk Track entrance, and carry on upstream for another 15 minutes until you reach the signposted Loop Track entrance.

It's worth dropping your pack here, and continuing upstream a short distance to where the stream narrows, emerging from the pinnacles themselves. Many hours could be spent exploring various gullies and wondering at these curious formations. The pinnacles – or hoodoos – consist of partially-cemented greywacke gravels which have survived the corroding forces of the Putangirua Stream. Many pillars feature an erosion-resistant cap, and some are thought to be around 1000 years old. Water and wind continue to work change on this very dynamic landscape, and you should avoid the area after heavy rain, when rockfall is not uncommon.

Pick up your pack back at the Loop Track, which climbs in zigzags through forest

Washpool Hut, Aorangi Forest Park

up to a wooden bench seat and lookout platform that provide a good viewpoint of the pinnacles. Higher up, on the main ridge, the Loop Track intercepts the Bush Walk Track on the main ridge. Take the Bush Walk Track in the uphill direction, and follow it until it reaches an old 4WD track on the ridge above.

This 4WD track leads across undulating terrain through regenerating forest dominated by manuka, and climbs gradually into mature forest. Lying wholly in the drier side of the Wairarapa, and influenced by the maritime climate of nearby Palliser Bay, the park's vegetation is different from the more mountainous and inland Tararua Forest Park. While beech covers much of the park's northern parts, here in the south mahoe, hinau and rewarewa dominate, with pockets of podocarps in lowland places. During spring, quite large areas of hillside erupt into yellow as the kowhai blooms, and the gullies often contain kiekie and nikau. Silvereyes, tui, tomtits and whiteheads are frequently seen, and on occasions trampers may hear the harsh kek-kek-kek of a New Zealand falcon.

The track climbs gradually, occasionally bursting out into small clearings that suggest a past history of farming. At one point there is a good view of the Rimutaka Range, forming a long brow above the blue of Palliser Bay. At a significant knoll, at about 700 metres, the track abruptly changes course from an easterly to a southerly direction, descends briefly to a dip in the ridge, then surmounts another low forested knoll. From here, it's a sharp 400-metre descent into the Makotukutuku (Washpool) Valley.

Dawn light on forest, Aorangi Forest Park

Washpool Hut occupies a small clearing on a level spot at the toe of the spur, set back from the river. A typical ex-Forest Service hut, it was built in 1962 during the height of the deer-culling, hut-building boom. The hut had rather a sketchy start, as a few years after its construction a large rimu crashed over the roof, just about destroying it. Rebuilt in 1968, the hut has survived for four more decades, and recently received a welcome spruce-up by DOC.

From the hut, a short track leads down to the Makotukutuku Stream. At first there's a pleasant open section, with toetoe growing on the banks – which during summer often flowers spectacularly. Beyond, the river narrows. Like many other streams in the Aorangi Range, the Washpool meanders in an unhurried sort of way, twisting through narrow banks that are never quite steep or long enough to comprise a proper gorge. There's only one point where trampers have to clamber around a rocky bank, although it would be difficult, if not impossible, when the river experiences a fresh. Watch out for ongaonga, a native nettle with a fearsome sting that is common in the Aorangi Range.

Mostly it's easy, pleasant river tramping. Lower down the river opens out onto farm-land, passes a private hut, and follows a farm vehicle track for some distance. For the last stretch stick to the river until it passes under the road bridge.